Loyal Audience

The Easy to Learn Guide in Building Loyal Audiences

By Simon Stone

© 2019 Simon Stone. All rights reserved.

About the Author

Simon Stone is a thought leader in content marketing and brand innovation. He has extensive field experience in marketing and sales in major multinational companies such as Omnicom, LVMH, Diageo, Benetton and Kraft.

Table of Contents

Introduction 1

Chapter 1: The Audience 5

   Who is the audience in the digital world? 6

      The Difference between Customer and Audience 7

      Why Should You Put More Attention to Audiences rather than Customers? 10

      The Audience Journey is more important than Sales Funnel 12

   Who and What are Loyal Audiences? 21

      The Two Types Of Customers 23

   Why is a Loyal Audience Important Especially Today? 24

      Key Communication Channel for the Future . 25

      The GDPR and Privacy Acts 27

      The Primary Supporters and Business Ambassadors 29

The Benefits of Having a Loyal Audience..........30

The Most Important Asset of a Business......32

Not a Cost Center but Profit Center..............34

Chapter 2: Loyal Audience is the
key to future business 37

How to Build a Loyal Audience?........................37

Process 38

Case studies..42

How to Maintain Your Loyal Audience? 43

The Examples 44

How to Expand Your Loyal Community?...........48

So what is a Loyal Community? 49

Ideas to Expand 50

How to Monetize a Loyal Audience? 53

Best Cases 54

Chapter 3: Building Your Loyal Audiences 57

How to Measure a Loyal Audience?..................57

How to Organize a Team for
Your Loyal Audience?... 61

    How to Transfer the Marketing Team to a
    Content Marketing Team?............................. 63

    Accommodating Marketing and Revenue
    Generation on Sales Functions 66

    The CMS and CRM 70

How to Build a Loyal Audience
Through Social Networks/Online? 71

Knowhow of each social media channels.......... 77

    Best Cases in Social Media Marketing 81

Why Content Strategy is Important
in Building Audience? 82

The Importance of Content Strategy
in Building Audience 82

Social Media Magic 86

    Facebook... 87

    The Guide in Creating a Decent
    Facebook Page 90

    How to utilize the marketplace feature.......... 94

The Different Types of Facebook Ads 97

Instagram 101

YouTube Marketing 116

Why You Should Be Marketing
On YouTube? 118

Making Money on YouTube 129

Pinterest Marketing 134

Additional Ways to Promote Your Site
for Wider Audiences 149

Introduction

The world right now is currently evolving as well that is why it is really important for you to take a grasp on the innovation that is happening in the present world. As you know, commerce in the past is actually superbly different from the ones that we have today. Imagine that in order for those people to sell their products and services they have to go from one place to another in order to market them. This actually puts a significant risk on the people that are doing it because their products might not sell and at the same time they will put a tremendous amount of money, time, and effort into doing such tasks.

Thankfully, we are in the era right now wherein we can do business right just in front of our computers or even phones! The good thing with online business is that you can actually do a lot in terms of niches without putting too much effort, well I am not saying that you will not actually put effort when you are doing business online but it is much less time consuming because you do not have to go from one place to another to get clients/customers thus you will just use the power of the internet to get them.

This is where the term "loyal audience" comes into place this is actually one of the biggest factors that you must consider if you are aiming to have a successful online venture journey. It can be really tough at first to build these loyal audiences because of the competition that is currently present in the online world. Building up a loyal audience will be your primary goal when you want to be successful in your online venture. When you are in your first online venture it could probably tough on what niche you will choose. This is also the time when you will need to determine what will work for you.

There are lots of choices to select from when you are planning to enter the internet marketing world. Some of the best examples of the niches that you can choose from are blogging, affiliate marketing, video marketing, and many more. To tell you honestly, all of the niches are profitable as long as you will have the ability to build a significant amount of loyal audiences and you must do it as quickly as possible because of the stiff competition that we have in the online world. So primarily, you must build your content well in order for you to keep these audiences loyal as much as possible. Aside from that, there are certain factors that you must consider in order for you to build them. This is why I decided to create this book to guide you all throughout when it comes to building loyal audiences because it is very important for you to plan your marketing strategy.

This book is loaded with various pieces of knowledge that you can actually use to make you win in this new venture of yours. By being extremely aware of internet marketing strategies you will have a higher chance of

INTRODUCTION

getting a deeper understanding of what you are doing. Right now, let us not delay the learning and let us deal with the topic of how to build loyal audiences in a more detailed way.

Chapter 1: The Audience

(Photo reference: https://pixabay.com/photos/audience-crowd-people-persons-828584/)

As the world evolves in technology, people's connectivity became easier, and a lot faster. Just one click, all information will be sent.

To study such complex things like the internet or technology can be a real pain in the head because it is a vast field to study on. It's because technology and the internet play a huge part in the digital business, or business in general nowadays because of the information that passes through different lines, business grows, and it becomes successful.

No doubt that it is because of the customers of that business but it is not enough for the customers or consumers alone to run or make your business successful because those customers might not be loyal at all and might not be beneficial in the long run that is why we will tackle how important those "audiences" to be loyal.

Who is the audience in the digital world?

Audience is a word itself that definitely states the meaning of it but when you say audiences in business it means that they are the people that will see things about your business, just like an advertisement from a brochure or a T.V. commercial and etc they are a huge part of the business industry, as they can help make your business successful because they will have the vision to make them grow.

CHAPTER 1: THE AUDIENCE

The Difference between Customer and Audience

(Photo reference: https://pixabay.com/photos/computer-laptop-technology-office-3368242/)

Although they may look the same in terms of meaning, they are two different things in terms of business. Customers or consumers are the people who are willing to pay you or for the product you sell or the services you offer. They are the ones who'll go to your business grounds or browse the internet to search for your business. They are the source of your money but not all people are your customers, always keep that in mind.

On the other hand, the audience is the people in general, as said recently, they are the ones seeing and setting up your business advertisements, banners, tarpaulins, recommendations and etc. These people will take up most of the numbers in your business, they are more likely larger than your customers. This is because before starting a business, you ask for recommendations right and try to look for advertisements, reviews, and other kinds of stuff to learn more about that product or service you want to try.

That only means, an audience is a potential customer. But if you'll summarize it all, businesses are meant for their customers because they are the main source of their money.

Remember this one, if your audience can become a potential customer, it is crucial for the audience to be numerous in order for you to have a higher chance of converting those audiences into potential customers. When making the message for your product or services offered, you have three choices:

- To make it look legit for your customer
- Make it look amazing for your audiences.
- Make it look beneficial for both sides.

For example, your business is car selling. Let's say that your company is well-known for manufacturing or even reselling sports cars then you made an advertisement which states how good your recently released car is, how fast it is how cool the design and other stuff.

So to conclude, your target market is the ones who can afford the car, millionaires and car enthusiasts. Now that you know your target market, let us say that for the first ten individuals to buy that certain model of newly released car by your company will get an incentive.

In this case, your business advertisement is actually legit for both your customers and audience, as for audience (your audience in this one will be the people who can't afford the car right now but hoping to buy one soon), they'll be encouraged in some way to invest in order to buy that car, with or without that incentive.

Therefore your business advertisement will be written or made for public release and there must be no words or things that can offend someone, making it a friendly opening for your business. It is just like welcoming people in finding out what you can offer to them or what is in store for them.

So to sum it all up, you should be cautious in making business advertisements, whether they will be posted on the internet or released in public because making an advertisement that is friendly is the easiest way to attract customers and audiences, even though the audiences are not really a fan of your product or service, they can still become potential customers in the future.

With the right words and procedures, you can work out your business smoothly and can be a way for you to be successful.

Why Should You Put More Attention to Audiences rather than Customers?

We are still on the top of this business talk, later on, we will go much deeper. So now, we are going to talk about why you need to focus more on audiences than your customers.

Before explaining much further, here is an example. Let's say that you are selling fruits and veggies in the market, and it is your first day of business. For the first few hours, people will just walk past by you but some will somehow look at the product you are selling, well in this case you have your audience.

Now there is this guy who bought an apple from you when you are in a market and there are a lot of people then let's say that this guy who bought apples from you becomes satisfied with what you are selling, then a few hours later, he came back with someone and told his friend that the apples you are selling are delicious, in return his friend will buy one.

That is the time when you are getting the people's attention around, they'll be curious as they see the two persons near your stall being satisfied with what you are selling. Then a few hours passed, your customer grew from one, then two, then now they are falling in line.

These people falling in line are once the audience and now becomes your customer, that's what we are talking about a while ago about the audience becoming a potential customer.

So there are people still out there just looking and hearing comments that your veggies and fruits are good, although some of them are not interested, the good comments from your customers will be in their mind, let's say if ever some of those audience knows someone who likes veggies and fruits, then they may suggest that there is a newly opened stall inside the market. Then the news will spread out like a virus until it reaches your new customers. Did you get my point? I hope you do, but don't get your hopes too high, I know it is exciting especially if you are that dedicated to starting your own business.

I am not saying that you should put all your attention and investments for your audience but what I mean is, as much as possible, when starting a business, try persuading audiences while getting loyal and trusted customers, in this way, even though your business starts small, with small counts of customers, the potential of it becoming well-known is through your audience.

To conclude, keep the balance between the two, make good quality products or services for your customers and a friendly advertisement for your audiences.

The Audience Journey is more important than Sales Funnel

A sales funnel is a marketing term that shows the journey of the customers in buying your product or affording your services offered. It is like a road map that varies from your potential customers (these are the people that heard about your business and are most likely planning to try out the services you offer or the products you sell), and next to that are the smaller number of people that are interested and wants to learn more about your business and a smaller one from these smaller number of interested people that might contact you directly.

But now let us talk more about the sales funnel because this thing is actually getting scarce, no matter how much you use this nowadays, it is not that effective anymore because it is supersaturated already but with the proper knowledge it can still be profitable not only that but it can bring you a tremendous amount of wealth.

CHAPTER 1: THE AUDIENCE

Although at some point in time where it is widely used it helped a lot of business in becoming successful, but keep in mind that the world is changing, evolving into something more advanced, and that thing also goes for business, in order to adapt and be able to achieve success in this evolving world, we must know or discover unique ways of running a business.

Plus, the sales funnel used to predict each and every move of a customer that is why it is commonly used back then, businessmen tend to know how to manipulate their customers or their business in order to keep it running and effective. But now, modern customers are very unpredictable because of the wide range of things you can afford right now and things that are newly introduced makes them unpredictable.

What is the audience's journey? It is like the sales funnel, more of a road map, but it contains a journey through your company directly in an interactive way.

It is also a guide for your customer to become a loyal customer, showing them that your business product or service can be trusted. Some audience journey maps contain actual feedbacks from recent audiences or customers who are now loyal customers of that certain business. In this way, the persuasion of other customers or audience will be easier.

Furthermore, if you can't predict the customers' next move then go with them and pretend that you are a customer of your own business or somehow act as a tourist guide, guiding your potential customers in patronizing your products or services, in this way, you can create your audience journey precisely and legitimate. This means that your business will be trusted by a lot of people who can see the audience's journey of some of your customers.

Although both ways show organization, the audience journey is by far the most effective way of getting loyal customers for your business. When making an audience journey, don't put too much complexity just keep it simple and easy to understand in a way that your business intentions are well-explained.

So are you ready to make your own audience journey map? Let me teach you some steps you can follow in order to make the perfect audience journey map.

1. Become one of them, put yourself in their shoes and try to look at your own business through their eyes. For example, your audience is a busy person and wants to prepare an easy and fast breakfast for the morning then create a content that shows an efficient way of making food or breakfast, it can be an appliance or an easy to cook food which all depends on your business.

   Although they say that this part is the hardest among others and by far the most costly. It will be worth it in the end, because at some point you knew how others see your business.

2. Find a triggering point in your business. You can do this by gathering knowledge about what makes your audience to look for information. In this way, you will know what to make for your audience. To do this, research words on a certain topic related to your business and then think of a way on how to make it a trigger for your audience the same way can be useful to them.

   For example, your audience saw something about kids perform well in school by following a good eating routine. Having said such, you must make a meal plan or guide of these certain foods they eat. In this way, you are driving straight inside your audiences' minds.

3. Figure out the things that make your audience stop making the move you want them to take. Like ask yourself these questions, why are they stopping from gathering information about my business? Then what are these things stopping them?

   An easy way to identify the factors that make them stop is to conduct an online survey, or if you have the time, you can talk to some of them personally. You can also base on the statistics made from your recent business activities.

   Here is an example, let's say that your business is selling packed meals or any kind of goods then your audience will believe that they are not that effective. So what is the thing you are going to do?

Go and contact an expert in that field, let's say a chef, a famous one or somehow influential and then make him explain that the packed meals you are selling are superbly delicious or tell them all the good attributes of it.

In this way, the chances of gaining the trust of your audience are from 0 to 98% or probably 100%. It still depends if that audience will stick in their belief that your product is not effective, but do not get to affected by that, because as long as the audience and customers are loyal to you are larger in number than those who do not support you, you do not have to worry.

4. Learn from someone that is an expert in the field that your business is included in. In this way, you will learn a lot of things about your business that you don't know about before. This is more of an advanced move to take but surely worth it because you will understand more about what your audience or customer really wants.

And by studying things about your business, also include tips and steps on how things work in your business. For example, your audience wants to learn more or is open to learning how to become a physically and mentally healthy person.

You must work with someone with experience when it comes to healthy living then ask for tips on how they executed it and etc.

In this way, you are like putting yourself in the place of your audience, and once you have learned all the new things in your business you can now answer certain questions from your audience you can't answer before.

5. Be the main source. Usually, your audiences will find your business through other sources. In those sources is where they will gather the information they need and then eventually those pieces of information will lead them directly to you, or your business.

   For example, let's say that your business is about party needs, the audience will most likely try to find the best and effective party needs they have to buy.

   Furthermore, spread out the advertisement directly from you to public areas or social media. In that way, it will be easier for you to reach out to your audiences.

6. This is the step where you must win. So now that your audience has gathered all the information he or she needs. Now what? Of course, it is normal for a person to have choices in life, so for your audience, it is you and their other choice of content and they will base their favored brand or business based on social media statistics and reviews because it is the most common nowadays.

This is why you must win these statistics and review then you will get a lot of audiences that will trust your business product or service. An example is, let's say that an audience is doubting whether to choose you or the other one in terms of information in the business you run (this business depends on what actual business you are going to establish).

What you want to do is start a partnership with other people or businessmen that specialize in advertisement and other stuff to make you pass the statistics and reviews.

7. Be creative. Now that your audience is accepting information from your content, they may still have doubts if any of the things in your business or services will actually work. In this situation, what you need to do is be creative. For example, your business is about selling different kinds of beverages, in order to increase your audience for your business, try making a video or commercial.

    Be creative in your own way and at the same time you think that will pass the people's general standards and by doing that, you are good to go.

8. Relate it to real-life experiences because now that your audiences are processing the information they have gathered from you, the doubts are still there. They might end up stopping their support because of insufficient encouragement.

What you need to do hear is very easy. Relate real-life stories that are connected with your business, for example, a customer that you ave changed his/her life is something inspirational. Not just you will get their trust but also you have encouraged them to live a positive life.

9. It is all about gaining the full trust of your audiences and making them spread the word. Now that your audiences trust your business product or services, it is now time for you to let them share your "works" (the advertisements and other pieces of stuff to make your business popular).

By this time, your audience mindset is convinced that you are really trustworthy and that all the things you said are legitimate. This will lead them to share your content with others, especially on social media sites like Facebook, Twitter, and Instagram.

10. Be in touch and continuously aim for improvement. You now earned your trusty audience. The thing that helped trigger the rise of your business is still running, and it is running very fast. So there are now only a few things you need to do and that is to ask them to follow you in every social media account you have, like Facebook, YouTube, Twitter, and Instagram. And to keep them on track, try updating weekly about the business so that they will have knowledge of new things

you are planning and new things that you have recently released.

11. Keep the relationship running. For an instance, for many months you have been running your business with the same audience and they are still growing and then one day they realized that they have gathered too much information and now it is time for them to let go because there is nothing new, it is just the same old thing repeating every day.

So the best thing to do in this situation is to think of innovative ways in reviving your relationship with your audience. Research things related to your business but something they have never heard of before in this way, you will regain your audiences.

12. Make something memorable. In business, you will gain and you will lose things. It is normal to lose your audience but you don't want to let them go without leaving a positive remark or even availing something on your business. Make something memorable that when the time comes that they will leave, make them answer surveys that will give positive feedback on your business product or service.

In this way, your future audience will know that before them, you had an audience that trusted you but sadly had to let go to live their normal lives, and also to venture out new possibilities.

Now you will not have a hard time answering your new audiences' questions as your previous audiences answered it for you already.

In business, trust is very important because it is one of the keys to having a successful and effective business. In gaining the trust of the people or the audience, you will need to exert a lot of effort, but surely it will pay off in the end. This guide on making an audience journey map will be enough in stating all the things needed in your business advertisement. Just keep in mind all the essential things you must follow in order to execute things easily and effectively.

Who and What are Loyal Audiences?

(Photo reference: https://pixabay.com/vectors/crowd-mass-people-shadows-306135/)

Now that you have an insight into what audiences are in the business world, let's dive a little deeper. Normal audiences are "normal", as they are the general people right? Then it'll stop there, if they will stay that way then they can be your audience now but tomorrow they will be someone's audience that's when the loyal audience will come in.

Loyal audiences are the ones you trust and the ones who trust you, your business product or your services offered. Most of the loyal audiences of a certain business had or has direct contact with the entrepreneur themselves.

Some of these loyal audiences are paid by the business owner in order to advertise their products or services to a wider range of people.

But there are some loyal audiences who are simply loyal and these audiences are big supporters of that business, maybe because they know personally the business owner or maybe because the business is inside their interests making them loyal to that certain business.

So whenever that you have started your own business, you should have a loyal audience, in this way, it will be easier for you to advertise and reach out to a lot of people who are interested in your business.

The Two Types Of Customers

Next is, let's discuss your customers. There are two types of customers in your business, your current customers and your potential customers.

Current Customers

Let's begin with your current customers. So who are your current customers? These are the people that buy and can afford products or services your business offers. They are the present which are the ones inside your business circle right now. They are the ones that keep the money circulating around your business. But anytime, your current customers might change their minds and go for other choices in terms of the business you run.

Potential Customers

This kind of customers are your typical audience, they may or may not become your customers, but that one depends on how good your persuasion is, or how much information you can give them from your business.

Even though your potential customers are not your regular customers, they are still important because they can make a huge change to your business status once all of them become your regular customers or current customer.

Influencers

Influencers are very important, especially in the digital marketing journey of yours. This kind of person is popular in social media or among the people that are using the internet. You want to have at least one influencer in your business because it will make your business known.

They are the primary key for your success, one word from them about how good your business products or services offered are, and then all the people that follow them will become interested in checking out or better, patronize your business product and service. Although, it is not easy to have an influencer (this is because some of them are costly) and it is truly worth it to have them.

Why is a Loyal Audience Important Especially Today?

Knowing these simple facts or people in the digital world can be a huge advantage among other businesses. Now you know how important loyal audiences are in the business world. Because earning a loyal audience will not only lead you to success, they will stick with you through the ups and downs of your business.

These people are for keeps, they have been there since the time you first started your business. So your success will also be their success in some way. That is why losing one loyal audience can be impactful to your business because they know a lot about your business and who knows if they might turn their backs on you that is why it is important to be careful and be kind.

Key Communication Channel for the Future

Communication is the key to success and it is true. Communication is one of the "keys" in succeeding in the business world. Without it, how will you send messages or important updates to people in your business circle? Learning how to communicate efficiently is one big advantage, this is because your business will be organized, loss in the track can be prevented, and all things will be in place just with the right communication methods. So how does communication work? There are four types of communication you can use or somehow follow.

The first communication type is "many to one". This kind of communication is like the other one that we will discuss later on, the only difference is that the message will come from different sources then will be transferred into a public communication field and from there, the message will be sent directly to the public.

The second type of communication is "one to one". This kind of communication is the most interactive among the other types of communication, why? Isn't it obvious? You will be talking directly to the person, one on one. You will do the negotiations with the client in person, you will be setting meetups.

But nowadays, you can also do this kind of communication without actually being there in person. Remember, the world is evolving through technology. You can now talk to the client online, either through chat or video calls, and actually, it is an advantage for both of you. Because both of you will save a lot of time and money in doing the meetings online rather than meeting in person.

Many-to-Many

The third type of communication is "many to many". In this type of communication, there are a lot of people involved, groups of people involved. There are a lot of communication channels in this type of communication, distributing the message faster than any type of communication, BUT, there will be times that the message delivered will be scattered. The advantage is that the message will be shared faster. The only disadvantage is that sometimes it is not organized.

CHAPTER 1: THE AUDIENCE

One-to-Many

For the last communication type, the "one-to-many", this kind of communication is the most popular and still widely used up to this day. This type of communication includes you the business owner or someone you can assign with to take care of all the communication services and all the clients wanting to invest in your business (or customer maybe).

What happens here is not that special, the sender will send the message or the updates to a certain field of communication service and then that message will be delivered to the receivers (clients or customers) directly. This type of communication is also the most reliable especially when you are going to make a public announcement.

The GDPR and Privacy Acts

In the GDPR or The General Data Protection Regulation is a law in the EU about the protection of data and privacy for the people of the European Union also known as the EU.

This law also applies to the distribution of personal data outside the EU and EEA areas. The goal of The General Data Protection Regulation is to let the individuals have full control over their personal data. But there are still certain measures followed in transferring data from inside the country to outside the country.

There are people, who control personal data, but before doing something to that data, either they are going to transfer it or read it, they must still follow the law about protecting the private data. There is a lot of process in handling personal data, you must ensure that the data will be safe and if you are the only one allowed to see it, keep it to yourself.

As much as possible, keep it all confidential as this will save you from breaking the law. And do keep in mind, that there is no personal data that can be processed unless the process is done in a lawful basis that states the GDPR, or if the person holding the data is granted by the law consent in processing the data.

It is also important to have a portable copy of any personal data from the data subjects. These copies will be collected by a data processor. Any data subjects have the right to erase their data in certain circumstances. Any businesses with activities that will circle around certain personal data are required to have a data protection officer or DPO, this person is responsible for managing the personal data and implementing the GDPR. In any case, businesses must report within 72 hours if ever there are data breaches. Those who violate the GDPR can be fined by about €20 million.

The Primary Supporters and Business Ambassadors

Besides having audiences, having proactive communicators, supporters and business ambassadors are major advantages. Here's why.

Proactive Communicators

Now that your business is expanding, of course, you will be having your own communication channel to deliver your messages in public, proactive communicators will do this job for you.

Keep in mind that they are different from influencers. These proactive communicators are daily updated on what's happening around your business, they are the ones who are delivering the messages directly from you then to the public or your business associates. They play an important role in your business that is why it is also important to take care of these people.

Supporters

Second, are the supporters, customers, loyal audience, influencers, business ambassadors, and proactive communicators are your supporters. Supporters are a general term for these people, as long as they patronize your business product or service they are your supporters.

Brand Ambassadors

For the last one, the business or brand ambassadors. These ambassadors are the human form of your business. They bring with them the virtues, the mission, and all the ethics of your business. They are the ones who will help you directly to bring up your business, they are like business partners but the only thing different is that they work for you.

They are also the ones managing some of your business branches. The thing notable from business ambassadors is their immense ability in promotional strategies. That is why having one, even though just one business ambassador can bring a massive change in your business status.

The Benefits of Having a Loyal Audience

Of course, in having a loyal audience there also benefits. These benefits will drastically help your business in becoming an effective and successful one. I will be listing down the benefits of a loyal audience in your business.

- By having large groups of loyal audience, you can compete with other businesses efficiently, why? From these loyal audiences, you can gather pieces of information that may help you improve some things in your business thus giving you the power to compete with others.

- You can effectively create campaigns for your business. With the help of your large group of loyal audiences, they can help you create campaigns for your business that will attract other potential customers in trying out or checking out your business.

- It will be easier for new customers to trust your business product or service. With the large visible number of loyal audiences you have, people will come to think: "Hey, this business is really legitimate." And when that happens, your customers will continue to grow, attracting and attracting others continuously.

- You will make lots and lots of money. From your loyal audience sharing your business with others, to sum up, all the benefits mentioned above, you will surely make a lot of money, making it easy for you to upgrade your business and then invest for further improvements.

- This is not much of a business thing but more of a personal one. Having a lot of loyal audiences can bring a positive vibe for you, you will be able to live happily and despite the stress, you are having in your business. You will come to think that you have a lot of supporters.

- In times that your business will fall down, your loyal audience will be right there to save the business with you. The loyal audience is not just supporters, they are also like family because they have been there since the start of your business.

- These are the benefits you can have by building large groups of loyal audience, even though you only have small groups, you can still feel these benefits.

The Most Important Asset of a Business

In business, it is normal to have an important asset. The most important asset in your business is not something you can hold with your two hands. It is not a data, property or something else –it is the people of your business, your employees, your customers, your audience, ambassadors, and all of the people that are involved in your business are the ones you should take care of.

When a business has a good grasp of their people, customers will easily trust their company. There are a lot of ways on how you can take care of your business assets. These are the tips on how to take care of your most important business asset.

Tip # 1: Make sure that you visit your business especially if it is a growing company and not only rely digitally upon if you have a physical store

It is important that you keep in touch with your business and its people. If you have free time, go and visit your company, interact with your employees, and radiate all positive energies around your company. In this way, you will maintain the health status of your business.

Tip# 2: Be an approachable person

There are a lot of companies or businesses that their owners are terror. They are driven with anger especially if they are stressed. Be the opposite of this person, even though stress is coming up your way, stay positive. Life is too short to become angry, sad or the likes of it.

Always be the one to bring the smile in your business or company, because remember this, you are not the only one stressing out but also your employees.

Tip # 3: Offer benefits in your company

It is a normal thing to do when your business is growing. Benefits are simple things that can make an employee happy and keep them motivated at work. Make sure to partner it up with a bright smile.

Tip # 4: Maintain a strong relationship with them

Building trust is essential, but what's more important is to maintain it. It is a great feeling if all of you in the company are working altogether in unity, with trust in each other. In this way, there will be no awkward situations or the likes of it, but all of you will be more comfortable working with each other.

Tip # 5: Succeed together.

Be a great leader. Lead the company and its people to succeed. In this way, you will keep your people intact and prevent them from leaving your company. Not just for your employees but also for your supporters and audiences.

Tip # 6: Be open.

If there are employees suggesting ideas, let them. Because not all things that make your company effective and successful only came from you but also from the people working in it.

Knowing these things can help you a lot in taking care of your business assets (the people). So always keep these things in mind when starting a business or if your business is already growing into a big one.

Not a Cost Center but Profit Center

For the last part of this chapter, we are going to discuss the cost center and profit center. So let's have knowledge first on what is Cost Center.

Cost Center is a part of a company that manages all the costs the company is going to pay. These include service departments, production departments, and administrative departments.

Profit Center on the other hand also manages a part of the cost center and also the profit from its departments or the company as a whole.

So what do these things mean for you? When having audiences, you should not spend more than what you can profit. Make sure that you have ways on how to make money from your audience, if not directly from them, but with their help. Because that is what business is all about earning.

Chapter 2: Loyal Audience is the key to future business

Now that we have discussed the basics about the audience in business, let's get deeper and tackle a specific topic, the loyal audience. As you know it from the recent chapter, loyal audience is mentioned a lot of times and you know that these kind of people are a very important part of your business.

Let's have a review. Loyal audiences are the people who have been there with you since the first day you have started your business, they know a lot of things about your business and together with your business running, and they are the ones helping you to be successful with it.

In this chapter, we are going to talk about the essential things you must know about loyal audiences, how to build them, maintain them, expand them and monetize them. So stay tuned and learn all these things.

How to Build a Loyal Audience?

Building your loyal audience is not that easy because it takes a lot of time, like really a lot of time and hard work. Because in building your loyal audience, the essential thing you are building is not the people themselves but their trust.

Process

You need to convince them to trust your business. So let's go straight to the point, how can you build your loyal audience? Here are tips on how you can gain your audiences' trust and make them your loyal and trusty audiences.

Tip # 1: Start simple

Starting in simple ways like posting positive and pleasing information about your business on social media can be a great start. This will partially give your audience that trust but not all as along the way, doubts will buildup on them, questions will be asked if the information that came from you is legitimate and can be really trusted. These doubts and questions may appear once you have built a large amount of audience in social media (general audience, not the loyal audience.)

Tip # 2: Be interactive

Now that you gave information about your business to your audience you must continue building your relationship, make that trust stronger. Be interactive, if you have the time, talk to some of them, online (or much better, personal) or you can create small groups that include your audiences, and there talk to one another.

Tip # 3: Be an expert in the field you are doing business with

What do I mean with this? Depending on what business you are running, make sure that you are an expert in that field. So it is very important to study the things related to your business, or if possible, aside from studying the basics, go and also study the advanced things.

In this way, the trust of your audience will build up, especially if you could let them see that you are really passionate and an expert in the business you are running.

Tip # 4: Create the right content and at the same time understandable

Of course, in convincing your audience, you should make your content exactly what your business is all about. You can put on some things for them to process in mind but not too much that it will lead them away from understanding what your aim is.

Tip # 5: Adapt to the present society in terms of creating your content

Connected with the previous tip, put some twist in your content, make them creative and based on the current trend. In this way, you are going to attract more audiences, especially millennial people. Develop certain business advertisement strategies you think best for the current generation.

Tip # 6: Observe the environment before starting

It is important to know the surroundings of your business. Is it safe? Is it stable? Can you maintain it? Knowing how your surroundings work can give you an advantage.

In this way, people will trust you more because you are not just a businessman doing business, but you are a businessman who knows how his surroundings work. Plus, it will give comfort to your audience if they know that the place you are doing business is safe.

Tip # 7: Maintain the right relationships

Have you ever wondered how to keep your audience loyal or continue to attract new loyal audiences? Most if not all, audiences based their preferences if the company has a good partnership with other companies. So if ever that you have partnerships and you are having a good relationship with that company then maintain it.

Tip # 8: Always check your e-mails

Updates from different sources must always be checked. This is a basic thing to do, everyday things are changing and updating, and in order to keep your loyal audience intact is to inform them daily updates on what's happening and what's going to happen in your company. In this way, the content will not run out and it will continue to circulate around the involved people in your company. And another thing that's note-taking in this part is that you have full control over it.

Tip # 9: Learn from your mistakes and accept feedbacks

We are not perfect. And so are you. Mistakes are made. As these mistakes are committed, it is guaranteed that you will lose some of your audience (but of course these audiences are not the loyal ones).

But there is a thing you can do to regain them back, and it is very simple. Learn from your mistakes. Mistakes open new opportunities. Make sure that you don't waste those opportunities. Feedbacks are also a great way of fixing or changing things in your business in order for it to become more effective and successful.

Tip # 10: Be patient

Building a loyal audience is not that easy. It will take a lot of time, effort, and perseverance. It brings a light feeling once you already earned your first group of audience and this factor will motivate you to continue your work. What more if you are already gaining a lot of audiences and not just an audience, but loyal audience as well.

Just by following these tips, you are ready to start building up your loyal audience. Although it will take a lot of time, it is very rewarding in the end for you and the success of your business.

Case studies

Now let us try another way on building your loyal audience. This time, through your business content that is why the audience will trust you through the content of your business this will commonly happen in social media sites where most of all the audiences can be seen. So here are the steps on how to attract a loyal audience through your content.

Step # 1: Make sure that the things you put about your business are not something you cannot really give

This one only means that all the things you put in your business advertisement can be given to your audience. Not only you are putting things to attract them but you are putting legitimate products or services in every business advertisement you are having. By doing this, you will gain the trust of your audience making them your primary supporters and then eventually your loyal audience.

Step # 2: Establish your own social media sites

Well if you are a busy man, you can pay someone to make and manage your social media sites but if you are starting small in business, it is best to create and manage your own social media sites. In this way, you'll keep in touch with updates and other things that may state potential customers for your business.

And not just that, people can directly contact you, increasing the chance that your audiences will trust you and will become your loyal audiences.

Step # 3: Make sure that the content you make is straight on point

If your business is about food, keep it on that specific delicacy you are selling or if it is food in general, at least group them. Organization in business is very important as confusion can be prevented which is not only for you but also for your audience.

These are the steps on how you can attract more audience in becoming your loyal audience through the content you post on your social media sites.

How to Maintain Your Loyal Audience?

So now that you know how to build up your loyal audience, I am going to teach you on how to maintain them, and prevent them from changing their minds and go on looking for another same business like what you have.

Like building up your loyal audience, maintaining them is not that easy. You will also need a lot of patience and effort in this one but ever ask this yourself: "Why bother if I can just make any audience loyal to me?

Absolutely, your loyal audience can be replaced by a new loyal audience, but don't you want them to stack up? Grow in numbers? Then the best thing to do because the larger the number of your loyal audience, a lot of people will eventually and will actually look forward to doing business with you.

Furthermore, keep in mind that the longer your loyal audience in your business the higher the chance you will have in succeeding in your business.

The Examples

The following are the methods you can follow in order to maintain your loyal audiences intact and have a healthy relationship with them.

The First Method: In going out in this adventure, bring your audience with you

Once your business has started and your loyal audience is growing you can set up the adventure to success and bring them with you. Whenever there are interesting pieces of stuff happening to your business, update them. In this way, their interest in your business will grow bigger and will attract a lot of potential customers.

The Second Method: Keep it running

It is not the business that should only be active at all times but also make it sure that you are putting time with your loyal audience. You should also manage the groups of a loyal audience you have. Like what I said previously, keep them updated on the happenings inside your business.

The Third Method: Don't change your goal

In the first place, why do you think your loyal audience sticks with you up to this day on your business? Of course, it is because they believe in the same goal you planned for your business that is the goal to success or this certain goal that keeps your business running.

Change in goal can drastically affect your loyal audience, making them think that you are not settled with the things you have planned for your business or company.

But if you will change something or add something in your main goal, inform your loyal audience, in this way they will not be shocked knowing that there will be changes in the plan. By doing this, you will still keep all your loyal audience.

The Fourth Method: Make sure to bring with you the best marketing team

There are a lot of factors for you to achieve successful businesses but the thing we are going to talk about is the marketing team. Having a great marketing team right behind you can help bring a lot of potential customers, customers in general, and audiences.

And by having this great marketing team can make your audience trust you easily and fully because they know that in any situation in business terms, you can adapt and deal with it together with your great marketing team.

The Fifth Method: Be sure to make things easier to understand

Nowadays, data and information are easily distributed. When making updates, advertisements, and the likes, make sure that it is easy to understand. It may be a small thing, but you should try looking at the small details it can give you. For example, what if one of your loyal audience prefer simplicity rather than complexity? Then you put too much in your message making it harder to understand. So what happens is that a loyal audience might end up getting bored or simply will not understand a thing about your message, ending up them leaving your business.

The Sixth Method: Communication is always the key

In business terms, we all know that there are a lot of keys that open new doors (opportunities). And no doubt that one of these keys includes communication.

Having a good communication line with your loyal audience is a must because, in long distances, communication is the only thing that will connect you two. So if you can, as much as possible, be in touch with communicating with your loyal audience.

The Seventh Method: Don't be afraid to let go

There will be cases that your group of loyal audiences will grow in larger numbers. So what does this mean? Time will come some of them will have doubts about what your business can do and start being toxic. Well, do not be afraid to let these people go, as they become what they are becoming, if you will still hold on to them, you are just going to bring down your business together with them. And having them still can put a negative impression for potential customers and a new audience.

The Eighth Method: Stay true to your goal

What makes your business great is its genuineness, originality, uniqueness, and authenticity, all words the same but that is what makes your business, your business. I know it is kind of redundant already but the point is clear I believe that I said it in the previous chapter that your loyal audience stays with you because you both believe in the same goal. So in maintaining them and your relationship to them, be united by one goal.

The Ninth Method: As the world progresses you must adapt to it

Let's say that you started off as a small business company. As your supporters, audience, and customers grow, make something that is new to the eyes and taste of the people involved around your business, but doesn't get too far from your main goal.

If there are new trends, try to fit them in with your business. In this way, you will attract a lot more audience and potential customers at the same time you will maintain your loyal audience.

The Tenth Method: Make events that involve your loyal audience.

Simple talks or a gathering can make a big difference in making your business successful. Orienting your loyal audiences can be a healthy way of maintaining your relationship with them.

So that's all the things you should take note of maintaining your loyal audiences. Simply following them and adding things that you think best can lead you to success in the business world.

How to Expand Your Loyal Community?

Now that you know how to maintain your loyal audience, let's step up to the next level. Let's go and expand the empire! Usually, loyal audiences come in small groups or sometimes they are just loyal individuals.

But can you imagine what might happen if these small groups and individuals gather together and grow into a huge community of loyal audiences ready to back up and support your business in every way possible?

I know that you are excited about knowing how but first let's start from the basics. Let me teach you some of the things that compose this large community of supporters.

So what is a Loyal Community?

A loyal community is a normal part of a business. These communities of supporters, customers, and loyal audiences are some of the keys you need to succeed in your business career. A loyal community is usually composed of small groups of loyal audiences you have since then.

They are alike branches put together to form something big, and from that something big, they will form branches that will spread out growing also into another kind of community? You get the logic behind? I hope you do, because all these business career talks is like guiding you (well, I am literally guiding you, but let's put it in a metaphorical way) in an adventure of a lifetime, telling you all these about these keys you will be needing to open the right doors that will lead you to your primary goal.

Ideas to Expand

Going back to the loyal community, I will teach you ways on how you can build and expand your loyal communities. So stay tuned, and process each word you are going to read, because trust me, all of these may sound simple, and yeah, all in all, they are really simple. But you can turn this simplicity into greatness by absorbing the right knowledge about these things.

First Thing to Do: Plan it all out

Before building your loyal community, you should plan things first, list the things you will need, the budget that you have, and other things you should have in creating your loyal community. With the proper plan, you will be doing all these things in making your loyal community clean and smooth.

Second Thing to Do: Find the right platform

In creating your loyal community, do not only create it in person, venture into social media sites and find the right platform for you. You can make a Facebook page, a YouTube channel or a blog.

It depends on what you think will fit exactly with your business run. Go on what's flexible and easy to access for you, in that case, it will be easy for you to stay in touch with your loyal subscribers and manage it.

Third Thing to Do: Set a mission or goal

You are not going to make a community without a goal right? Because it is complete nonsense having a moving group without a destination so when making a loyal community, have a reason why are you building it, give your loyal audience something they will believe into until you reach your primary goal. In this way, establishing your loyal community will be easy.

Fourth Thing to Do: Expand

Let's say you have built your loyal community, now what? Go on and expand that community into communities. Appoint leaders from your main loyal community that will establish and manage the next loyal community that will be created. In this way, you are in touch with that loyal community without actually being there. This can save you a lot of time.

Fifth Thing to Do: Give reward to the loyal audience that does a great job in your loyal community

Noticing the works of one of your loyal audience is a kind thing to do. It means that you appreciate the things they do for your business. Just by giving a simple reward can make them happy and become more motivated in what they are doing for your business or growing company.

Sixth Thing to Do: Explore new ways in maintaining your loyal communities

Now that your loyal communities are expanding, time to make ways on how to maintain your loyal communities strong and growing. In order to do this, always be creative, venture out new possibilities because you know, we humans are eager to explore a lot of things.

If you are going to put up new things in your loyal communities, people will not get bored and will be driven by their excitement and curiosity in the new ways you have discovered.

Seventh Thing to Do: Be an understanding leader

It is important that you become a leader people will look up on to. I am talking about this in general and not just in business terms. Because once you started in making your first loyal community, you will be the one who's going to lead it.

And expect that, all things will not fall into place always there will be times that it will go down, but don't lose hope with that factor. Always stand up and show your loyal community who is the boss!

To sum things up, all of the previous up to this chapter, things you must do to achieve success in business is not that easy, and it's true when they say all good things come from hard work and not an easy work.

To shine on top, you need to climb, and before you start climbing, you are the one who will be making your own stairs. These stairs are of course composed of your supporters, loyal audiences, customers, and the loyal communities you are going to establish.

As far as I know, a lot of people fail before coming up top, so don't worry if you fail many times. It is okay to get frustrated at times but doesn't let it consume you. Give yourself time to fall, and prepare to rise up again. That is why you have your loyal audiences and loyal communities; they are the ones that will help you rise up again, that is the purpose why I am teaching you all these things about succeeding in the business world. It is not always about money, fame, and success. It is all about living a life and not let the business itself eat you.

How to Monetize a Loyal Audience?

If you already built a large number of loyal audiences then go and celebrate your triumph. Building large numbers of loyal audiences is not that easy, and it is something that other businessmen can never achieve.

Monetizing your loyal audience is a thing. Let's say that, yes they are your audience but not all of them are your customers. You are giving them free content of your business that is why they are expanding.

So ever think of making money from your loyal audience? This will be not that hard to do but also not easy, it is just placed in between those two. Then you have the trust built up already, what are you going to do now is the process of monetizing them.

Best Cases

Of course, you will be doing this on the internet, the digital world. Here are some common ways on how to monetize your audience:

- Make a product that you can sell online.
- Start promoting the products of other people.
- Start a social media platform.

Now you are getting the idea of how you can monetize a loyal audience. So basically, how can you monetize a loyal audience?

Your audience is there for a reason, and that is because they are unified by your cause. Your business interests them. These causes, ideas, interests and other pieces of stuff that unifies them is something that you must understand or know. In order to monetize a loyal audience, you need to understand what they want. Ask them don't be afraid to approach them.

In this way, you will know exactly what they need and what they want. Then right after, create this certain thing or product your loyal audience wants. Take note that once they grasp on it, your loyal audience just turned into your customers.

So now that you monetized your loyal audience, the next thing to do is maintain that product and updating it or changing some of its attributes depending on how the world or your loyal audience changed.

Another way to monetize your loyal audience is through social media sites, especially making blogs related to their interests. If you want to know if your monetizing is successful, ask for feedback. If you get positive feedbacks then it only means one thing. You have succeeded in monetizing your loyal audience.

You can also make subscription models. This is a sure way that money will generate from your customers or audiences. This is because they need to pay a price in order to access the content of your business or buy a certain product or provide a service from your company.

Chapter 3: Building Your Loyal Audiences

I know that we have tackled this in the previous chapter but what's new on this chapter is that I am going to teach you an in-depth guide on building your loyal audience. There are a lot of things you must know before diving straight in building your loyal audience that is why you must pay attention to every single detail from this chapter. Let's start.

What does it take to build loyal audiences? Of course, the loyal audiences themselves, the things they are interested in, your business, and your plan on how you can build them up.

How to Measure a Loyal Audience?

In this chapter, you will know who is your true loyal audience and the ones who are literally audiences, that right after they'll just go away.

Let's focus more on the details on how you can build your loyal audiences. Again, ask this to yourself: "Why should I focus on my loyal audiences?" Remember the things you have just read in the previous chapters and then we can continue.

It is very important to build up your loyal audience and not just acquire them. Some of these people are not really "loyal", some are just bystanders pretending to be loyal ones.

Are you surprised to know these things? Like said, it is not easy out here and in fact, these things we're discussing are the hardest part of having loyal audiences.

Here is an evolution of an audience into becoming a loyal one or a loyal customer in your business:

They all start from being a stranger until they are attracted to what your business can give them or benefit them especially if it will fit in with their interests. Most likely they will know about your business because of business advertisements, social media sites, or simply from a recommendation from a friend.

Then next is after these strangers knew a little information about your business, they will finally check out your business (they are now called visitors). They will most likely view it online from your social media sites. In this case, not only they are gathering information from your business, but you can also gather information from them. It is like a give and takes scenario.

These visitors you have will become leads. With the help of your loyal community, you can gather these visitors' information through your online site registration and subscription pages. You can also contact them if they gave you their contact number or e-mail.

CHAPTER 3: BUILDING YOUR LOYAL AUDIENCES

Now that you have the right and enough information about these visitors. You can now organize them and then with proper managing skills, these visitors will eventually become your customers.

Once these newly acquired customers are satisfied with your service, they will eventually become your loyal customers, or best, become promoters of your business product or service.

They will start making positive statements and feedbacks about your business which can help attract more strangers with the same interests as them. And after attracting them, the cycle of a stranger to a loyal customer or audience will repeat.

Let's say your loyal customers and audiences grew large in numbers, how will you measure them? Publishers from your social media sites (these publishers are one of your assigned leaders that came from your loyal communities) will base the numbers on the comments, the likes, shares, and how many times the social media site or the web page is viewed.

There is a term used in measuring the loyal people in your business, this is called 'Engagement' or 'Engagement Rate'. So here is a situation, let's say that there is an individual who finds your Facebook page and then he or she likes the post about your business there. And then that's it, and he or she never returned again.

This means that this individual showed a good engagement rate, but they are just visitors and they didn't remain loyal to your business. Remember that not all your engaged visitors are loyal visitors.

Here are four ways on how you can measure the engagement rate of someone who visits your business sites or pages:

First Way: Keep track of the new visitors and the returning ones.

New visitors will most likely put up a good engagement rate if they just visit you. If ever that they return because they are curious or interested in your sites' content then the engagement rate will rise up drastically.

Second Way: Measure how much time these visitors spend on your sites or pages.

This means you are going to measure the engaged time your visitors spend on your sites or pages. Usually, interested visitors will spend hours and hours reading the content of your pages. So keep track of this, it is also essential in measuring the engagement rate.

Third Way: Recirculation Rate

The recirculation rate will tell how many visitors read an article and then transferred to another article on the same page or site. If the engagement rate is higher, that only means there are a lot of visitors engaged on that site or page.

Fourth Way: Check if the visitors finished reading an article.

In this part, re-read the article and check out if how many visitors read an article fully, by half, or just the introductory. There you will know if they just scrolled down into your sites or pages or if they actually read your pages' content.

These are the common ways of measuring the engagement rate of your visitors and I hope that this will help you someday when your business grows big time.

How to Organize a Team for Your Loyal Audience?

Knowing how loyal audience work and building them up can give you an advantage in business terms. Let's say that you know all of these factors because it was just previously discussed. Now what we are going to do is organize them, create a team where you can assign them what to do or where they belong.

Organizing a team for your loyal audience will also take a lot of time and effort but it will eventually pay off, giving you an organized group of people. In this way, you'll prevent messes in your loyal audiences' groups.

Here's how you can organize a team for your loyal audience:

Step # 1: Again, plan it all out

Like building your loyal community, the same thing goes with organizing a team for your loyal audience. You need to plan things out before trying out any move in organizing the team. Build drafts or anything that will help you out in preparing for the organization of the loyal audiences' team.

Step # 2: Get all the support you can have

A little help can do something, but great support can change everything. Always keep that in mind. Get all the support you can but remember to ask for it in a nice way. You might be surprised at what support you can get, you might get more than the support you expected. With these supports you can get, it will become easier for you to organize your loyal audience team.

Step # 3: Talk with your loyal audience about organizing them.

It is good to have the consent of the loyal audience you are going to organize. Although it is a good thing to organize them, it is still better to talk to them about it. Because by doing this, you'll increase their trust in you and your company.

Step # 4: Take action from your plan.

Now that you have your loyal audiences' consent, it is time to make all the plans happen. Start by grouping your loyal audiences equally and then assigning one leader in each group. Right after, assign them to a designated place where they can attract more potential customers. By doing this, you are going to expand your audiences and potential customers drastically.

Step # 5: Keep in touch

Once the organized team of loyal audiences started in their assigned locations always be updated on what is happening on the groups or teams you have organized.

Planning it all out and putting it in action seems difficult. Yes, it is not easy, but if followed carefully and correctly, expect massive changes in your company. And benefits will come your way and not only you but also for your customers and loyal audiences.

How to Transfer the Marketing Team to a Content Marketing Team?

Having a marketing team is good, and yes it is a must-have in the business. But, not all your profit will come or will be based on your marketing team. And that is where the content marketing team will go in.

Content Marketing Teams are the group of people that both came from your original marketing team and then transferred on this new group or the people you assigned straight to this content marketing team.

So what is a marketing team? A marketing team or a marketing department is the group responsible for promoting your business. Their main job is to do research on effective and strategic ways on how to improve sales in your company or business. They are also the ones responsible for finding potential audiences or customers. They research their backgrounds, their interests and many other things that can benefit your company.

On the other hand, the content marketing team is like the marketing team in terms of promoting your business. But they are more specific on promoting actual audiences and potential customers your marketing team or department founded. They are the ones responsible for social media promotions. And also I forgot to mention that they are also responsible for finding strategic ways on how you can improve the company or business, and not only the business but also its people (the audiences, loyal audiences, customers, supporters, and potential customers).

Let's say you are building a content marketing team for the first time. So how are you going to transfer people from your original marketing team into your new content marketing team? Here are steps you can follow in order to transfer them organized and smoothly:

Step # 1: Know your employees' skills.

Although the marketing and content marketing team share the same job, Content marketing requires more interactive skills because, in this department, your employees will most likely interact personally with your potential customers and audiences. That is why it is important to know each one of their capabilities if they can take on the new job.

Step # 2: Prepare the new content marketing team's place.

Before transferring people from your marketing department to your new content marketing team, make sure that you readied the whole new department or the place where the people from your marketing team will be transferred.

Step # 3: Start transferring in small groups.

If ever that your company has large groups of employees, especially in your marketing department. You need to start slowly in transferring your employees. Start with small groups and then slowly transition all of them into the new content marketing team.

Accommodating Marketing and Revenue Generation on Sales Functions

Marketing and revenue are two words that actually come along really well. How did I say so? The primary reason is that if your marketing strategies are very effective rest assured that everything will go well and you can expect that you will meet your target revenues at the specific dates that it is expected.

However, things only get rough whenever you are ineffective at your marketing strategy especially at the initial stages of your campaign.

Let me give you an example, for an instance you are an affiliate marketer and you are using CPA as of the primary medium of your campaign marketing then you might as well look for places where you can market your campaigns.

There are various mediums that you can choose from on where you can post your campaigns in CPA. Though you can opt in to use the freeways in order for you to profit there is a lesser chance for people to see your campaigns.

For example, you have chosen Facebook for you to market your campaigns. You have the ability to join groups, create Facebook pages, or just post it on your profile.

That was one of the primary mediums of internet marketing before it became supersaturated and the moderators of Facebook had prohibited the inclusion of such affiliate links on their site resulting in A massive ban on the accounts.

But when it is still tolerated by Facebook, lots of affiliate marketers particularly the CPA marketers have profited from it. In fact, some of them (the hustler ones) are earning more than a thousand dollars a day just by posting links on Facebook. If you do not have any idea of what CPA is, the meaning of it is "Cost Per Action" it means that there is a specific campaign that you will promote online and you will get a compensation for each leads that you will get.

But wait what is "leads" by the way? It is a term used in digital marketing to describe the individuals who took action on your campaigns. Since digital marketing is not only catering about selling products to get a lead because CPA is all about everything from answering surveys, filling up email link building forms, and etc.

So once an individual goes to the landing page you will accumulate views and after that, if they take further action such as buying a product, filling up surveys or forms, and etc. that views will be counted as leads already.

But before we talk further, maybe you are wondering on what is the meaning of a landing page. It is actually a webpage in which that the offer is landing, it is very important because once you utilize the landing page really well then it can contribute a lot in your profits.

We just talked about one example of it which is CPA and with regards to that digital marketing is a very broad topic especially when we are talking about revenue generation.

So I will give you another example to help you another stand more about the correlation between marketing and revenue generation, especially in the digital world.

Another example that I can give you, is affiliate marketing in terms of selling physical or digital products. In this way, you will act as a middle man or agent but in the manner of everything is done online. So the logic is the main website, for example, Amazon.com is selling a specific kind of product then the next thing that you will need to do is to market it by means of posting the affiliate links on social media sites, creating your own review blog, and etc. On every sale that you will make if the buyers bought from the links that you posted you will earn a percentage from it.

To tackle the ways in how internet marketers make money from their affiliate links I will discuss it in a more specific way on the bulleted points below.

- Social media posting – the social media sites that I am talking about here are Facebook, Instagram, Pinterest, but not only limited to that because a lot of people are also using various sites such as Yahoo! Answers, Quora, Reddit, and many more.

Most of the marketers pretend that they have already tried the product and posting on various threads on social media or creating their own posts of the benefits of the product and putting the affiliate link there.

- Tube sites –the most popular approach of guys in the internet marketing world that are very well-versed in creating video content are review videos. In this way, the marketers will create video content that focuses on describing the product itself. It is just like enticing the prospects to buy the products that you are reviewing.

- Website/blog creation – this is a very effective way to showcase your products because you will have full control of the content that you can put in it. Since social media and tube sites have their own set of rules expect that you cannot have all the freedom in the world to post what you want because you might get banned. This is the primary reason why a lot of internet marketers resort to it because they want to gain full control of their content.

Those are the most famous ways on how you can market your affiliate links. Now you have an idea of how marketing and revenue generations go along with each other. Omitting one of those will not make your digital business in any way that is why it is important that you will make yourself aware of these two factors on your sales functions.

The CMS and CRM

Let's begin with this topic. First, let us start with CMS. What is CMS? CMS or Content Management System is the one responsible for all the contents your company or business is making. Content Management System varies from 'Web Content Management' and 'Enterprise Content Management'. The web content management manages all the contents of your business or company in your social media sites or web pages. The enterprise content management, on the other hand, manages the entire content straight from your business or company.

Now we'll discuss the CRM or Customer Relationship Management.

In this management, their main job is to manage the direct contact of the company or business to its potential customers, audience, or the business partners of your company. To manage any human asset in the company, this management uses data analysis in order to keep track of an individual's history and then they evaluate it if it can be beneficial in the company's success.

Customer Relationship Management uses a lot of communication mediums like emails, telephones, live chats, web pages, and social media sites.

It is important to understand what these two kinds of management can do and how they are essential in your company. You must also know the difference between these two kinds of management.

By doing so, you will have a much more organized way of doing your digital business.

How to Build a Loyal Audience Through Social Networks/Online?

Digital marketing became much better and easier nowadays compared to the early onset of the internet because websites before tend to be very passive compared to the sites today that are really interactive.

For example, the sites before are only using very basic HTML functionalities which makes marketing very hard back in those days. Thankfully, websites evolve day by day which makes everything easier. You will just put pictures and content on the post then integrate the affiliate links there then wait for the money to come in.

However, it does not mean that money will just come in after building a website or blog of your own because what you need to do to make your campaigns productive is by having loyal audiences.

But the question is how you can build a loyal audience?

It might sound really complicated and difficult but it is easier than what you actually think. A loyal audience in the digital world can be acquired by means of various techniques. Although, it takes time before you can build a loyal audience of your own because of the competition that we have in the online world.

Do not worry because we will tackle those techniques below and put it on a beginner's perspective so that you will not have any hard time in understanding it even if it is your first time to engage yourself in digital business.

Here are some of the most notable ways to build loyal audiences real quick:

- Useful content – this is the most important way that you can build loyal audiences. Since people are looking for content that they know that will help them with regards to what they want to achieve, they do not want people fooling them that is why if your content is not that useful and the primary purpose is just to fool people just to buy your products or getting leads from your affiliate links then make sure that your content is legit and useful.

- Continuous content production – it is also useless if you have a very informative content but in the end, you will not post any content on a regular basis. This will make your audience lose their interest on your site because they are seeing that you are not that active.

So be sure that you are having a good amount of content on a regular basis so that you are assured that your audience will keep on wanting to read your content increases your chances of getting conversions(leads).

- Put some cliffhangers – this is a very important way to make your audience to keep going back on your site. Once, you put a post on your site see to it that in the end, people will expect to read the continuation of your post on another day which will give you another source of traffic on the following days because people will keep checking your site for your new posts. Aside from that, there are some of those audiences that are too lazy that is why what they do is just to subscribe to notifications with the use of subscription buttons.

- Subscription buttons - Furthermore, you should not overlook those subscription buttons because those are very useful in building loyal audience. Those subscription buttons will help you out in building an audience base which will let you share a lot of content which highers your chances of turning those traffic into profit.

- Consistency – there will be a time wherein we will not see that much traffics on our site that is why you must keep your head and hopes high and not give up. This is where people fail because once they are seeing that the site is not materializing than it supposed to be, they are not determined anymore to continue that is why they left their site hanging for nothing wasting all their hard work and effort.

- Create some viral content – this factor actually happens when you are lucky enough to post content that captured the eyes of many people. This will give you a significant amount of traffic that will give you an opportunity to profit a lot. However, before content becomes viral it must be shared by thousands or even millions of people but this must not be the reason for you to lose hope because viral contents are pure luck and you must not rely on it completely. However, if you want to higher your chances of having your content go viral, one trick that you can do is to have a catchy title and photo.

- Have some freebies to your audiences – this is a very common way on how you can build a tremendous amount of audience on your site. The freebies can be in the form of physical or digital products. In this way, people will be enticed to visit your site from to time and it is always better to have traffic because it can increase the visibility of your site in search engines.

- Hold giveaways in the form of raffles and contests – in the blogosphere, giving out giveaways through the form of contests and raffles. A lot of bloggers collaborate and plan on what giveaway would they give to their audiences. They usually share the prizes that they will give.

  For example, there is this blog that wants to host a 1000 USD raffle with the use of the Rafflecopter app. If the said blog does not have the capacity to host such a large sum of money in a giveaway then the owner of the blog can seek help from other bloggers of their own niche if they can put up some contributions for the 1,000 USD to be completed.

  For an instance, they were 4 blogs that agreed to have a giveaway then most probably the 5 bloggers (including the host) must give in 200 USD each and in return, their names will be put in on the giveaway post which can give those sponsor blogs an exposure. In return, that exposure can also bring some traffic to their blogs as well making them benefit from it.

- Mailing lists – have you noticed that almost all of the blogs that you have browsed probably has their own mailing list subscription form? The answer for that is simply because mailing lists are made to have browsed probably has their own mailing list subscription form? The purpose of the mailing list is for the owner of the blog or website to send updates on their subscribers. So in short, mailing lists are created for people to subscribe and get notifications on their emails on what's going on to their site.

See? Building loyal audiences can be intimidating at first but once you have done the techniques properly rest assured that you will be on the right track.

To give you an idea, it was really difficult and I have to be honest with that especially when I created my first website. It was really tough because I have to experiment and go through the different trial and error in order for me to see what works or not that is why I have gone into different ups and downs when I was still starting out.

As time goes by I realized that it is a part of the process especially when I became successful. This is when I have known that it is really crucial to fail first because it will teach you where you have gone wrong and correct it accordingly so that you will become successful the next time around. That's what happened! After I fail several times I have managed to correct my mistakes and optimize my campaigns for them to become more profitable.

I found a way to create effective campaigns to build up loyal audiences real quick. To be honest, all of the techniques that we have talked about are very effective, they might sound basic but I tell you that they are all worth it.

CHAPTER 3: BUILDING YOUR LOYAL AUDIENCES

Knowhow of each social media channels

Social media right now is getting really big that is why it is a great way to promote whatever digital business that you have. The social media channels that we are talking about here are Facebook, Twitter, Instagram, Youtube, Pinterest, and many more.

Once you utilized these social media channels rest assured that your target profits will be reached in no time. However, be sure that you have the knowledge of the different knowhows when it comes to promoting your business on social media channels because one wrong move can actually ruin your campaign and can waste your efforts.

For you to avoid those pitfalls we will discuss the different know-how on bulleted points down below.

- Do not overdo everything – this rule is very important especially to social media channels that are heavily moderated such as Facebook. It is a must to keep things in a gradual manner because you might get ban if you overdo things such as posting links. It is also prohibited to post links that are very obvious to be affiliate links. Some of the digital marketers previously used cloaking sites to hide their affiliate links so that the moderators of Facebook will have a hard time determining if their links are purely affiliated.

However, as times go by Facebook became more intelligent because no matter how hard you cloak your affiliate links they will still have a way to detect it making your account ban in just a couple of hours or even minutes!

This is the primary reason why a lot of internet marketers are very reluctant right now to use Facebook because of that factor. But there are still very brave internet marketers that are really innovative because after Facebook has changed its policies particularly when it comes to posting links. These guys have used their blogs as a landing page instead of directly posting the affiliate links to trick the moderators and not let them know that you are already posting your affiliate links.

- Create a catchy title – this is very crucial especially if you are aiming to get your business going because people will tend to click more on those links if they will get curious about it. One tip that I can give you is that you must always put a title that will tempt the people to click on it by not putting all of the details on the title so that people will wonder what's inside of that link.

- Interesting picture – this factor is very important as well because it will let your audience know that there is something on your content that they must know. The most common thing that digital marketers put on their photos right now particularly

CHAPTER 3: BUILDING YOUR LOYAL AUDIENCES

on the thumbnails that they put on their YouTube videos is the question mark. It seems like it is a very simple symbol but it actually works a lot in enticing the viewers to click on the video.

Since YouTube is a very popular medium nowadays for marketers to make money online that is why instead of just being a mere marketer by means of writing they transform themselves into video content creators to market their products and not only that they also get a lot of profits from YouTube's ad program specifically Google Adsense.

So keep your thumbnails or photos at check before you decide to post your content.

- Join exchange like groups – as we all know organic traffic particularly to your social media pages can take time before it happens that is why it is important to take some action on it by joining different liking exchange groups. In this way, you can accumulate a lot of likes in no time which will eventually help you get a significant amount of viewers in no time. This will help you to quicken up the process of getting a decent amount of audience.

- Be truthful – this is the most overlooked knowhow when it comes to digital marketing in social media. Since you have all the freedom to reach the audience from all over the world, some marketers tend to abuse it that is why they post contents that are fake and misleading. Most probably, people will fall for it but I tell you, that kind of strategy won't work for the long term because people will go away immediately after their first transaction on your site.

- Avoid putting prohibited links or content – before posting it is a must that you read the policies of a certain social media site so that you will be aware of what is prohibited to post on their site. By doing so, you will not have any problems when you are already done posting your stuff because most probably if you violate the terms of the site you are just putting yourself in an untoward situation. Imagine that you will get banned after you have finished posting your content/link wasting all of your efforts for nothing.

- For YouTube always make sure that your videos are 10 minutes long – if you are into YouTube video marketing then make sure that your video is in the 10 minutes and up range. By doing so, you can have the capacity to put as many ads as you want for maximum profit.

- Get that content coming – be very aware of when will you post your content because regular basis posting is a great way to give your site some visibility in the search engines.

Those are simple yet efficient knowhow if you want to have a rewarding digital marketing career. Since social media promotion is really crucial for your business to grow always keep those tips in mind at all times before taking any action.

Best Cases in Social Media Marketing

You can only say that you are successful with your social media marketing if you are seeing the results that I will enumerate down below.

- The traffic of your site is significantly increased after starting your campaigns and you can also find some leads already.

- Your site has been indexed already into the search engines most especially Google. You will know that you are successful if your site gets indexed on the first page.

- You are seeing repeat visitors. This is very important because when you see that there are repeat visitors, it only means that people are very fascinated with your content which is really a good thing.

- A lot of your views are turning into leads, in this way you will eventually profit from your site so that you can have some ROI from the efforts that you have made.

Why Content Strategy is Important in Building Audience?

There is a saying that goes "content is king" especially when you are into websites and blogs. Since content is the one that the audience is looking for because it is where they can learn things you must ensure that you have a very decent content strategy that you can implement every time.

This is where a lot of web marketers fail especially the new ones because they are just making content without even knowing if it is feasible or not. This results in the closure of their business without even having a glimpse of any sales or leads at all.

Furthermore, all kinds of organizations or private people that have websites must possess a great content marketing strategy for those individuals to endure the stiff competition that different business boasts nowadays. It is a requirement for you to know your aspirations and execute them effectively.

The Importance of Content Strategy in Building Audience

Why are you producing content and who is your target audience for it? In this part, we will tackle it further so that you will have an idea of what content marketing strategy really is. But the question is how a content strategy can be effective and why it is so important?

To give you an idea of what good content strategy is, you can actually refer to the bulleted links below so that you will know how important they are in digital marketing.

- It will make your business known – an effective content strategy will make your website or business visible to the major public.

- It costs less - content strategy is all about hunting your possible clients digitally, producing the need and urgency to purchase your services or what you are selling as it tells you about your reputation to your possible clients. There is a study that depicts that advertisers turn into online marketing because it can reach a wider base of the audience compared to the conventional way of advertising.

- An efficient strategy possesses a definite knowledge of your audience, what gives them the urge to buy something, the place on where they reside, and their personal info such as their gender and how old are they. This data supports you produce content that is really enticing to view.

- Since you have a good content strategy, rest assured that it will give you a higher chance to accumulate wealth by having a good conversion rate of views to leads.

- Your content will be much more optimized because content that underwent poor planning will definitely result in the low quality of a post.

- A keen detail to stating the story of your business - if your content does not imply that there is a reason that people must invest in it then it is a must to recreate it once more and give it another try. You have to state your journey into different stages such as being ahead of your competitors so that you will have an edge among them which will make people visit your site.

- An amazing content strategy gives you the privilege for your audience to notice your content and give them the motivation to disseminate your content with their networks on various platforms. Your content must load them with numerous pieces of information about your site so that when someone asks them about your site or business they will have an answer which will give your website free publicity.

As a result, you will notice a tremendous amount of people viewing your website and transforming into loyal audiences or even clients. As your traffic increases, search engines will notice that you possess amazing content for their users and for them to get their presence back on your site from time to time.

- Putting some credentials as leading A-site in the vicinity of your niche with a content strategy, you have the capacity to answer the inquiries that individuals have. The reason for this is that you spent time and effort to take a grasp of your audience and the content they are looking for.
- In the extended term, you will be able to put yourself as the deciding factor in your niche. When people give you this confidence, they rapidly take in your product and advertise them offline.

To conclude, content marketing strategy is a crucial factor that puts spice to content marketing. If you remove that factor it resembles a person that is firing his gun without any targets at all just firing it all out, entirely uninformed of the numerous possibilities that it would have had if it is aimed at a specific target. An excellent strategy supports you to produce and arrange your online content in a manner that it suffices your present audience and be noticeable to your future audiences.

But how do we get a good content strategy?

- Get a topic that is aligned with the season – when you are into this factor there is a higher chance that your content will be noticed and the best-case scenario will go viral which will result in better statistics.

- Be realistic – avoid fooling your audience because it can actually hurt your audience base in the long run because if people found that you are just playing around with them then most probably that they will just walk away and leave your site.

- Keywords are the key – by getting the right amount of keywords integrated on your site, you can surely become visible in different search engines in no time leading to increased traffic.

- Never ever plagiarize – search engines nowadays are really intelligent most particularly Google because their algorithm knows if you just copied your content from different sites that is why it is important to check your content first before posting it and as a matter of fact-checking of plagiarism is actually super easy and mostly free on some websites. Just be sure that the site where you will check your content is legit to ensure that your content will not be stored on that site.

Social Media Magic

In this module, we will discuss each popular social media sites that you can use to start your digital marketing career and how you can utilize them for success. For the first one let's start first with the most popular social media site today which is Facebook.

CHAPTER 3: BUILDING YOUR LOYAL AUDIENCES

Facebook

(Photo reference: https://pixabay.com/photos/social-media-facebook-smartphone-763731/)

If you are just starting out with internet marketing then it is a must for you to try marketing on Facebook. It is probably the largest social media site in the world because there are a billion users that visit it on a daily basis.

From a kid who just wants to take selfies to people that are doing other stuff such as business and just merely conversing with their peers, it's transformed into a primary site to grow the business of different industries.

Although, there are lots of scandals and issues that Facebook faced a few years back they stood tall and proved that no one can stop them from their vision. This advantage of Facebook in marketing will not actually deteriorate easily because it innovates day by day.

In this module, you will know the fundamentals of Facebook marketing and use it to your edge. This instructional is targeted at a newbie level who wants some fundamentals to marketing their enterprise either big or small on the most prominent social media site globally.

Ask yourself if your audiences can be found on this social media site?

Before we tackle the various techniques on the different ways to make profitable campaigns on this site, ask yourself if your targeted audiences are the ones using Facebook?

Here are the things that you can utilize and begin marketing through the use of this site.

Utilize the pages feature

The most utilized FB marketing tool that people use today is FB Pages. Like a profile for own use, it is actually storage of data of your business no matter what niche you currently belong to.

The people that use the site can follow and like the page, which will make them acquire updates from time to time to be visible on their Facebook accounts.

Some fanatics even follow the page or subscribe to it so that they can see the updates first when that certain page posted something. However, marketers cannot fully utilize this one because there is a new feature that is created by Facebook for them to monetize their users at their side. So they had this sponsored feature (suggested pages) which allows the marketers to reach more audience but in return, they have to pay for a certain amount of audience that they wanted to reach.

So when you are successful getting the likes of audiences, it's a nice resort to suggest to subscribe to you so that they can see your posts much quicker. It will spare you from spending too much cash in the extended period so that you will not have to use the sponsored feature post frequently.

There are several dissimilarities among the regular profile and fan page. To link with an individual as your own profile, you will have to accept the request that is given to you.

When you have a fan page, individuals can subscribe to you so that they can see your posts quickly.

Another disparity is that there are no bounds to the number of individuals that can subscribe to your page. If you possess an account for your sole use you can just possess a maximum of 5,000 friends on your account which is the complete contrary of pages.

The most exciting portion of pages is you do not have to pay for it before you use it because it is totally free. The creation process is super hassle-free as well.

But the disadvantage is, it is very difficult for a page which does not possess a popular brand to get noticed.

However, you can higher that chance if you will make a very decent-looking page. Do not worry because I will guide you all the way to achieving that goal.

The Guide in Creating a Decent Facebook Page

The worse scenario is that a lot of organization does not utilize this social media site to their maximum capability. The bad thing is that several organizations utilize them way below average which compromises their reputation. These points will support you in committing such errors.

The picture on your profile

You should consider putting your logo on your profile picture which is located at the upper left corner of your page. On the other hand, the cover photo is somehow dissimilar because you have the freedom to choose what you want to put there well it depends on you.

"About" section

This part is situated below your profile picture. This is a way for you to introduce your business to your possible loyal audiences. Just only put the important information there. However, right below there is your information section in which you can put as much information as you want.

Elaborate on what your business is all about and your distinction. If possible spend some time to compose some informational content so that people will be enticed to view your page.

However, if you are too busy you can just mimic the content that you put on the about page of your own site. Just see to it that you put content on the basic info of your Facebook page.

That's it for digital business, but if your business has a physical store equivalent then you must ensure that you will also put your opening hours and the days that you operate.

Put a not so formal and conversational tone in it so that readers will be more enticed to read it.

Only put useful content on your timeline

What you put on your timeline will be seen by your audience, just like when you post stuff to your own profile.

See to it that what you are putting there is all informational. Don't post updates frequently about similar content and always make sure that you do not post fake news.

Here are examples of insights for the different kinds of stuff you can post to your timeline:

- Connects to articles that have the same niche as yours
- Backlinking
- Amazing innovation of your products in your posts
- Freebies

Furthermore, see to it that your posts are very catchy and informative. Then do not overdo content posting just like posting numerous times per day because your audience might get fed up.

Flooding is one reason for your subscribers to unfollow you. If what you do is just post all kinds of stuff that just obviously promote your business then it is also a red flag for your subscribers.

But prior to posting tell to yourself if it puts up some usefulness to the topic.

Know the metrics of your page

Facebook Insights will give you the ability to check your analytics so that you will know where to adjust. Check them very carefully. If you saw that there is a large flow of traffic on your page know what is the post that causes it so that the next time you post an update you can use that strategy again to experience such huge traffic.

Utilize different groups and marketplace

Recently this social media site has integrated lots of features for various kinds of pages.

These are some ways that you can utilize to boost your organization's presence.

How to promote the use of group feature

Before there is already this feature however it is enhanced more throughout the year that's why it became a very useful tool to promote whatever business you have.

It is a requirement for you to have your own page for your business then you can have your own group to get more traffic. This acts as a monopoly over the group because you can put in your logo or banner on the cover photo.

This feature is the same as to the different communities that you can find online but with extra features that will spark up your traffic.

You can create groups with the same niche as yours to get possible customers.

The amazing thing about this feature is that it does not require you to pay for it. Users tend to engage more in this kind of community because Facebook is widely used throughout the world.

To make your page organized you have to visit it from time to time to know if there are comments or inquiries that you should respond to.

How to utilize the marketplace feature

If you are aiming to sell something then the marketplace feature might be the best one for you. It is the same with the usual buy and sell site but has a much larger audience base.

It is one of the latest features that Facebook is still developing to improve it more. If you are planning to be a merchant (buying and selling stuff) then you should set up a shop instead to reach more buyers.

After you put them on Facebook, your products will be visible when people search it using the keywords that you put in it. This is the best strategy that you can use if you are in the commerce niche.

Aimed Marketing

This great social media site gives you this great privilege to aim at your prospects in a specific way.

You can produce ads at a specific factor that you wish to optimize your ads more so that it can reach a wider array of audiences. It also gives people the chance to conceal ads that are undesirable to their taste.

Since it accumulates demographic information that depicts the activities of your users, this social media site possesses the most prominent ad programs.

You can aim at people depending on something that you can view in their profiles, as well as get to know your success with each portion.

Ads can be executed depending on the preferences with the use of views or actions (PPC or PPI). This social media site will let you view the various bids, for you to have an idea if your bid corresponds to the present bid. You also place everyday limits so there will be no instance of you going way ahead of your budget.

The amazing thing about these ads is that they are superbly strong and has a higher probability to materialize because they are made and modified by an expert team that focuses on aiming ads based on the cookies of the users.

However, the main con of this is that it is very costly. It is rapid to implement numerous ad campaigns but be sure that it is used the correct way because you can lose a lot of cash if you are not mindful about it.

Facebook Ads

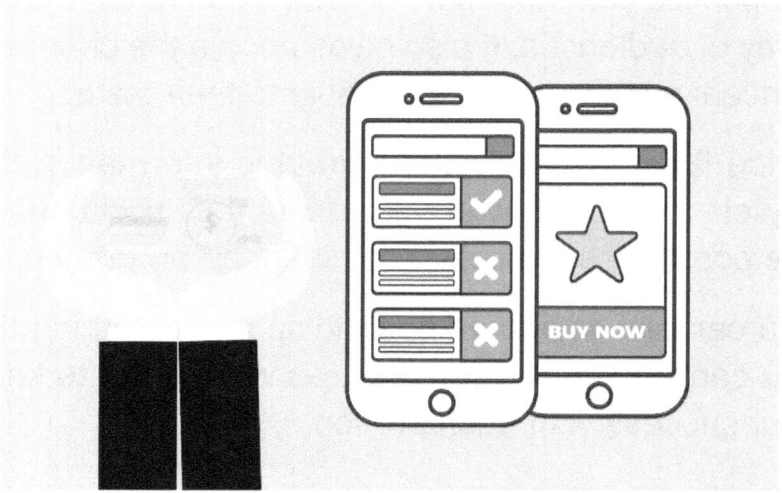

(Photo reference: https://pixabay.com/illustrations/ads-mobile-click-advertising-4050225/)

There are lots of ads that you can select from such as passive pictures, videos, rotating ads, and many more.

One of the best strategies that you can use to know what kind of ad you should place is by knowing your competitors.

To have a fresh ad campaign, it is a requirement for you to possess an administrator account. After that, you can browse the ad manager in which you can set up your campaigns.

It is pretty complex at first but eventually, you will get a grasp of every feature once you familiarized yourself in it.

CHAPTER 3: BUILDING YOUR LOYAL AUDIENCES

But the most important thing is for you to get the basic functionalities first and learn each of them carefully.

The Different Types of Facebook Ads

Here we will have a brief discussion of the different Facebook ads that show up on the site so that you will be aware of how to use it to your advantage.

> Video ads – this is probably one of the most common ads that we can see on Facebook because most of the time we use to watch a lot of videos on that social media site. The advertisement pops up for a certain period either at the beginning of the video, the middle part or at the end of the video.

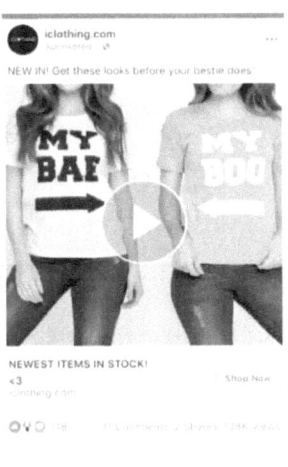

> Image ads – this type of ad is scattered all over the site and one of the most common as well second to video ads during this time of writing. You can find them mostly on the right side of the Facebook webpage in the form of square images with captions beneath

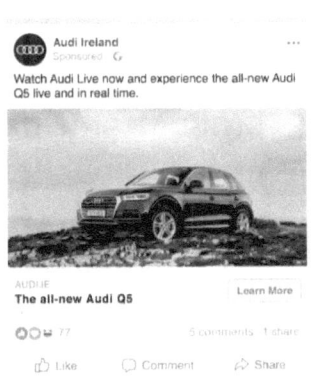

them. However, if you will view it on mobile it will appear in the center as well the same as the stories in the newsfeed.

> Slideshow ads – this is actually one of the recent developments in Facebook ads. It is a combination of video and image ads the only difference is they appear mostly at the center and has an arrow for you to change ads or wait for a certain period in which the ads in slides will change automatically.

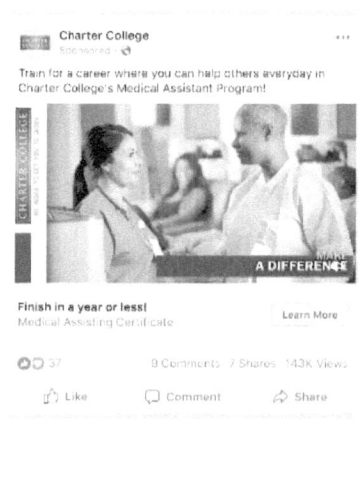

> Collection ads – because of the rise of e-commerce nowadays Facebook has integrated a nice way in order for them to showcase the products of their advertisers along with the picture of the product and price. The ads usually appear at the center part while you are browsing your newsfeed and it links itself to the website of the advertiser.

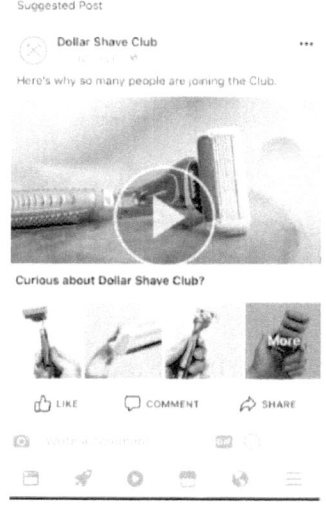

CHAPTER 3: BUILDING YOUR LOYAL AUDIENCES

- Post engagement ads – this is where the Facebook pages of the advertisers are showcased. The posts of the advertisers appear just like the normal page posting of non-sponsored pages so that it will not look like it is a paid advertisement allowing people to click on it without realizing that it is an advertisement making the audience reach much more effective.

- Lead generation – for affiliate marketers this is the most utilized one because it allows them to reach audiences to sign up on their offers much more efficiently to increase their earnings more.

(Photos reference: https://www.facebook.com/business/ads/ad-formats)

Strong Aiming Options

As I have stated previously, this social media has several strong aiming tools for any online ad program.

You can aim by checking the profile of users. You might start with the area if it is crucial. You can be more specific by having a profound knowledge of the other info such as zip code, province, city and etc.

This can be perfectly utilized for small businesses in the area. From there, you can select the different info you can use for your campaigns.

Aside from that, you also can aim audiences by knowing their likes. For instance, you have services that aimed at sports fanatics. You can put sports in the "Interests field" or probably you were a writer or a book worm you can put there "reading or writing books" as your interest.

Facebook also allows you to aim at specific personal e-mail addresses. So if you possess an email list of individuals that you want to aim, you can use the ad manager feature to aim at those individuals.

The Bottom Line

This social media site is not only strong but it is flexible as well. No matter what kind of organization you manage, it has sufficient marketing selections that you can optimize your marketing strategies to suit the different factors of your campaign.

Knowing all the features will definitely take a while for it to happen, but once you did it you will have the utmost power that you can get as this social media site is still innovating at a very quick speed and on a daily basis it transforms into one of the best assets in digital marketing.

Although there are still lots of controversies that Facebook faces mostly about data privacy concerns that are thrown into them but rest assured that it is the safest medium that you can use right now.

If you are not still using this medium, it is a must that you should consider it. Think of your campaign first and attempt to test out some things.

Instagram

(Photo reference: https://pixabay.com/photos/instagram-social-media-web-pages-1519537/)

There are times that when you are browsing your newsfeed on Instagram you can see a lot of posts that are completely irrelevant and you are wondering why it is still lurking there?

These are the following reasons for that:

- It garnered almost a billion monthly users
- The adult population on this social media site is more than half the entire number of users
- A large number of users are not US-based
- It is known that Instagram is already becoming like Facebook in terms of user interaction because users of this social medium tend to like at least one organization on their account.

It's known that Instagram is not only for own use and fun anymore. It is currently a platform that is used throughout the world that gives organizations to put content, widen their organization, sell pieces of stuff, and motivate their subscribers

The good thing with the users of this platform is that they are very active. Although it just started to be just a picture and video sharing software it transformed itself into a social media site like Facebook and they were successful with it. The higher number of users visits their IG accounts multiple times a day which makes it a very desirable way to market your business.

Instagram can support raising knowledge about products as a huge number of IG users have invested a lot of time in checking out the different products that are available on the platform. It also gives you the power to show off your products and services in a genuine way without forcing people to buy them.

Maybe you now have the urge to jump on the IG's bandwagon but you might be uncertain of how you can start it off. We know that IG can be pretty hard to use if you are new at it, and that is the reason why we are tackling it on this part of the book.

IG Business Account

Before we start, it's crucial to keep in mind that this platform is made for quick content. To keep you on track with your audience, you will have to spend time and post updates on a regular basis.

Then make your IG profile updated, and you will have more interactive and happy subscribers. With regard to this, we will further dig in on how to have and uphold a triumphant IG profile.

The Setting Up of Account

If you execute an IG app you will possess two options for the account creations process. It will tell you to either manually sign up or you can use your FB account to connect it. See to it that you create it using a corporate email so your IG profile will not be connected to your own FB account.

Then you have to put in the details of your account. Take note that you must enter your real business name so that your followers might not be misled when they typed in your business name of the search bar.

The name of your business can be actually different from the username always remember that but you can place a username that has a resemblance with your business name. Always choose a username that is extremely readable. One advice that I can give you when your business name is already taken is that you can use half of your business name so that it will still be recognizable especially to your repeat customers.

Unleashing the Full Potential of Your IG

Now it's part to select the proper profile photo. Your profile photo is a huge portion of the notion of your first-time visitors. That is why you must ensure consistency regarding your photo.

Make sure that you are utilizing your logo or other kinds of a photo that relates to your brand.

The IG Settings

In your settings, you will have the ability to edit your password, notification modification, and your other activities. Here are some of the important functions you should see immediately.

In the "Story Settings," you can modify who can view or reply to your stories. It is a must to change the settings to public so that everyone could see it and increasing your chances of having a good online presence.

The Most Effective Method To Create Videos For Social Media

Sorts of IG Posts

Since you have made your record, it's a great opportunity to begin posting content with substance. IG gives you the opportunity to post a few kinds of stuff including photographs, recordings, and stories.

How about we talk about the diverse types of IG posts and some recommended procedures for empowering commitment that will result in remarkable outputs?

Pictures

The most widely recognized post on IG is a picture post. When posting pictures, it's critical to share an assortment of photographs. Different photographs will demonstrate your image is various and can connect with your subscribers in various ways.

It's additionally critical to recall that IG clients are searching for interesting posts from brands, not obvious outright ads. Attempt to catch your organization's culture with a way of life in and out of photographs. Abstain from posting such a large number of photographs of your item because it might just feed your subscribers up.

In The Background Posts

These posts offer a look into the piece of your business that individuals don't typically observe. It's significant that they don't look organized — in short being legit is critical!

Reposts From Employees

Extraordinary posts can be directly before you or on your representatives' IGs. Just do not forget to credit the first person who posted it. Reposting photographs from your representatives is a simple method to minister legitimate posts and take your business to the next level.

Instructive Posts

Instructive posts offer quick tips on the most proficient method to do or make something. The photographs or recordings generally present the directions in a manner that is speedy and simple to pursue.

Influencer Posts

Influencer posts are one of the most popular types of posts in IG to utilize the notoriety of a public figure to advance your image. These posts regularly incorporate a visual of the influencer utilizing or connecting with your products or services. One of the principal advantages of influencer posts is people believe them much easier because the post came from famous people.

Inspirational Posts

An inspirational post consolidates a straightforward visual with a motivational content. These posts support your group of subscribers and enhance their respective self-esteem. They are mostly shared by IG users because they inspired them and want to inspire more people with it.

Client Generated Content

Like representative reposts, client-generated content is a type of content from your subscribers. Your labeled posts and posts with your image hashtag are an extraordinary hotspot for client-generated content.

Sharing your fans' and supporters' photographs not just makes the initial impression feel better, it likewise demonstrates that you client-generated care about your clients. Simply make sure to acknowledge the first post for a tag or in the subtitle. To repost client-generated content, screen capture and yield the first post or utilize a reposting application like "repost" for IG.

News Jacking

It appears as though there's a "vacation" for everything nowadays. Occasions like Christmas and St. Patrick's day produce a huge amount of impressions because it is like a trending day. Participate in the enjoyment by taking part in a neighborhood, national, or world pattern. A newsjacking post is an incredible method to post clever substance that catches the eyes of people.

Instagram Photo Size

Since we've investigated what you can post on IG, we should check out a few ways to ensure your post is fruitful. In contrast to other internet-based life stages, IG's straightforward profile design compels you to concentrate on the nature of your post and not the amount.

While this needs extraordinary commitment, it additionally implies that you can't take the post for granted. Accordingly, it's imperative to utilize high reso pictures on your IG feed for better satisfaction of your audience.

Square pictures ought to be 1080 x 1080 in resolution. Scene pictures ought to be 1080 x 566 in resolution and profile pictures ought to be 1350 x 1080 in resolution. Notwithstanding what size you transfer, each picture will appear as a square in your profile feed.

CHAPTER 3: BUILDING YOUR LOYAL AUDIENCES

How To Take Cool IG Photographs By Using a Smartphone?

(Photo reference: https://pixabay.com/photos/phone-photography-camera-mobile-802125/)

Maybe you might think that you should have the high-end camera to take the best picture? Then you are incorrect this time because telephone camera innovation has turned out to be progressed to the point that it presently matches thousand-dollar cameras.

Stunning photography is never again restricted to those with expert cameras. Any person can take eye-getting photographs your subscribers will love utilizing an instrument that you have the capacity of buying.

Here are the ways that you can use to take astounding photographs that you can put on IG.

Utilize the standard of thirds

To quickly improve your photograph organization, turn on your camera grid lines. Expect to put your subject at the crossing point of one lot of vertical and even lines. This system, known as the standard of thirds, is famous among painters, artists, and picture enthusiasts.

Setting your subject in a skew makes a slight unevenness that gets your audience's attention.

Concentrate on a solitary subject

It's occasionally said that a picture taker's responsibility is to make straightforwardness from turmoil. A jam-packed photo with different subjects in an edge just occupies from the focal point of your shot. It can even amaze your group of spectators.

Rather, center around a solitary subject in every photograph. Expel diversions by editing them out or finding a spotless foundation to shoot against.

Search for fascinating points of view

Individuals are accustomed to seeing the world from eye level. To make fascinating and new photographs, amazing photo enthusiasts ordinarily use shots from alternate points of view.

Switch up your shooting point of view to catch an elevated view or worm's eye perspective. The examination with various points is used to discover new viewpoints on basic sights.

Influence evenness and examples

The human eye is normally attracted to balanced shapes and items. Some of the time, it's ideal to defy the norm of thirds and focus the scene on your edge. Driving lines are another progressively explicit type of balance that maneuvers the eye into the photograph.

Individuals are additionally attracted to designs. An example could be artificially-made, for example, a tiled floor, or common, for example, petals on a bloom or vines. To make things truly intriguing, separate the example with your subject.

Utilize characteristic light

Standard overhead lighting makes brutal shadows and features that make undesirable dull and light regions in your photographs. To keep this from occurring, utilize delicate characteristic light at every possible opportunity.

Take a stab at taking photographs alongside a window, and for outside shots, the half-hour before the sun rises and after dawn regularly offers the most striking lighting as the sun is low in the skyline which is truly breathtaking.

Exploit negative space

Negative space is the unfilled space around your subject. Leaving negative space around your subject will attract consideration regarding the ideal focal point of your picture and keep it from looking swarmed.

Note:

(When you transfer your modified photograph to IG, it will naturally trim your photograph into a square-shaped object. To transform it back to the first width, press the symbol with the two outward confronting bolts.)

At this stage, you can include extra IG channels — however, don't go excessively insane. Each Instagram channel has its own character that can definitely change a photograph.

Next, have a go at modifying your photograph lux. As indicated by IG, "Lux adjusts the introduction and gives genuinely necessary splendor" to photographs. Lux make can make your picture increasingly energetic and bring out subtleties. To do this, press the sun symbol at the highest point of the screen and alter the level.

Make any last changes utilizing Instagram's modification tools. Press the edit button to alter your photograph's aspects.

Footages

IG gives you the privilege to put some footages of your own as long as they are only short-length. You can get professionally modified footages from your PC or smartphone software.

Footages in IG play immediately without emitting any sounds just like on Facebook. This is why see to it that at least the initial part of your footages don't require sound to be familiarized. You can utilize your description of the video or give an alert to your audience to turn the sound on.

Boomerangs

Execute your IG then click the camera button in the upper left-hand edge of the initial screen. This is a built-in software camera. You can also enter it with the use of doing a swipe motion on the right side of your screen.

See the settings on the lower part of the screen. The default option, to which the cam sets in to capture still pictures it is where you will notice that the initial option to its one side is Boomerang, which captures 3-second, looping footages that run either advance or replay.

Instagram Stories

Instagram Stories enable clients to post at a higher recurrence without over-posting and obstructing your feed. Stories normally include less-organized, progressively natural pictures and recordings. Like FB Stories, this IG stories eventually disappear after a couple of hours.

Stories are about genuineness. While your Instagram feed should highlight cleaned photographs, Stories can be somewhat cruder. Utilize the component to give an idea in the background take a glance at your image or relate it to your products and services.

Furthermore, offer photographs and recordings Stories are likewise an accommodating device to exhibit live occasions your business has.

The Use of Hashtags in IG

(Photo reference: https://pixabay.com/photos/analytics-hash-tag-hash-social-2998837/)

Hashtags are very popular in the internet world which is popularized. They are the keywords that are typed after the number sign and they do not have spaces at all. They are specifically utilized to share important happenings so that more people will see it.

How it is Utilize in IG?

Instagram feeds are not dormant which is common because there are approximately almost 100 million pictures are disseminated on a daily basis. With that number, it can be hard for your account to leave an imprint.

On IG, they compile posts from various users into one feed. Although only accounts that are public can be visible when looking for them.

IG provides no hassle for people to look for their tagged content. It is further divided into 3 portions which are the related ones, top ones, and the latest ones.

For example, if you have the urge to tag your post then you can use the hashtags #ballgames, you may want to tag related hashtags like #basketball, #volleyball, #baseball, or #football to widen up your audience.

YouTube Marketing

(Photo reference: https://pixabay.com/illustrations/youtube-marketing-affiliates-3152186/)

This subchapter is filled with helpful and easy techniques as it can support you in building your own channel from scratch, and it can also give a great marketing plan that all marketers of skill level can learn from.

We will tackle how you can create one of your own, producing and modifying your footages, how to think creatively with the latest techniques, money-making strategies, and putting ads and everything.

CHAPTER 3: BUILDING YOUR LOYAL AUDIENCES

Prior to tackling the much-advanced topics let us tackle the fundamentals first that every marketer should understand prior to getting themselves in action. To be honest this is the most important part that you should concentrate on even if you already possess an existing channel.

But before we end this Instagram topic, the question is:

"What types of ads are there on Instagram and is it worth it to utilize them?"

Actually, the ad types of Instagram resembles completely like Facebook that is why when you are already aware of the different ad types of Facebook then you will not have any problems at all in familiarizing Facebook ads.

Why You Should Be Marketing On YouTube?

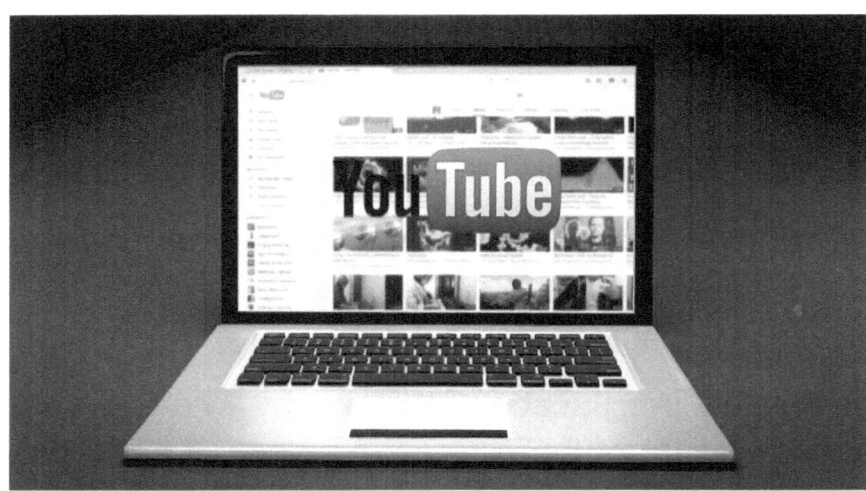

(Photo reference: https://pixabay.com/photos/youtube-laptop-notebook-online-1158693/)

There are numerous advantages of marketing on YouTube that many enterprises take for granted.

The initial one is a little bit obvious. The use of footages right now is really effective. It is the epitome of marketing, and if you are not still using it, you will surely be left behind by your rivals.

YouTube has a tremendous and various group of audiences, which cheerfully utilizes both YouTube's and Google's own robot crawlers to discover posts they're searching for.

In case you are ready to enhance for the correct keywords, you will have the option to interface with that group of audiences immediately, rather than trusting a Facebook Ad appears in their channel.

This enables them to discover a larger group of audiences, which joyfully utilizes both YouTube's and Google's own web search tools to discover posts they're searching for.

In case you're ready to go for the correct keyword you will have the option to interface with that group of audiences quickly, rather than trusting a Facebook Ad appears in their channel. This enables them to discover you, not in a different way.

Since YouTube recordings can appear right off quickly in Google's indexed lists and YouTube is the second most usually utilized web search tool after Google, you need to have this enormous advantage on your side.

Since there are only little companies that use YouTube on their campaigns you will have a sure definite advantage when you utilize it!

YouTube Demographics

(Photo reference: https://pixabay.com/vectors/accountant-counting-calculation-1794122/)

When I state YouTube has an enormous and various group of audiences, I am serious about it. They possess over 1 million interactive users, and the site accumulates approximately half a hundred million impressions on a daily basis.

We realize that YouTube's audiences observe over 3 billion hours of video consistently and more than 1 billion video watch hours on a daily basis.

We additionally realize that portable video medium is expanding tremendously, yet this is particularly valid for YouTube—and people want to watch everywhere to go making the website really flexible; the normal session usually run for about 40 minutes on YouTube, which is super plenty that is why you must aim for a content that will be perfect for versatile audiences.

YouTube is Completely Innovative Medium For Digital Marketing

So if you want to be triumphant with your YouTube campaigns then you must approach it unique compared to its rivals. Other social media companies spin around both making and imparting incredible substance to the objective of making mindfulness, commitment, and discussion.

I don't think this is the manner by which why many people use YouTube. YouTube posts are super similar to blog posts because you have the capacity to integrate. Without a doubt, individuals will have the privilege to comment on your videos and they have all the freedom however if you feel that there are already lots of negative comments about your videos then you can actually turn off commenting.

YouTube Updates

Throughout the years, the expansion of this video sharing site became really abundant. This is the primary reason why they see to it that they improve their features as much as possible which led to amazing results.

Here are some of the most notable updates that they have done:

- Mobile users can rewind or fast forward the videos

- You can adjust your screen size and resolution according to your device and specs

- The inclusion of banners and flash ads on the videos for people to monetize their videos

- Uploaders of the videos can remove the remarks on their videos with the censoring option.

Now we know some of the significant improvements that have been made for the betterment of YouTube then it is now time to know how to enhance your own channel.

How to Modify Your Channel to Your Advantage

It is actually a requirement for you to set the options of your channel accordingly before starting to post videos. However, if you already have an existing channel you can still modify it.

I will help you get started by discussing it further below.

Produce your Own Account for Your Enterprise

Create a channel that is aiming towards your enterprise. Especially if you have an established brand you can name the channel straightly towards you for people to see it. You will acquire more possessions in that manner and people will subscribe to you and check your channel from time to time and this is proven.

Graphics: Adding Up Some Creativity

You have to put two photos one for your profile and for the cover picture. You have to select these photos properly because people will see them beforehand and they will leave a first impression on them.

This is just like hitting two birds in one stone if some of your subscribers from other platforms go to your channel, it is a must that they can see that it is really you. This also ensures that it is your legit account that the subscribers are clicking and not just another poser.

For your design select a thing that comprises your enterprise while being catchy and professional. There are lots of free software available online and offline that you can use to create designs. They possess presets that are made to suit your channel correctly, all of which can be fully modified. Just try to make everything look professional so that it will not be undesirable to look at. You can put in some text content to add up more comprehension to what you want to imply.

Contact Info and URL

The aim of YouTube marketing is to redirect them to your site or landing page. Make it more quick links to your channel. They will be viewed in the lower right-hand edge of your channel art, in a location that is super accessible.

To accomplish it, you can go to the "edit links" button.

You can also add your own personal or business email so that your subscribers will have the chance to contact you. You can also add some of your social media account links.

The Description of Your Channel

Many just take this for granted and believe me that it is not a good idea to underestimate it. An excellently produce description content gives you the ability to tell your audience why they must patronize your content. It will help you explain what your business is all about so that they will have a concrete idea of it.

Featured Video is the Key

Channels must completely have a featured video. This video will be situated at the lower portion of your channel. When your audience takes action, it plays automatically which will surely mesmerize the viewers. This allows you to select your preference for telling all about yourself to the audience. This is super crucial, for the reason that there is no description of your enterprise on the starting page.

Let me reiterate this once more just use this footage to give your audience the idea of what they can get from you.

Content Uploading

If you already have a channel then the next thing that you want to do is to upload videos. You can actually see the upload button on the upper right corner of the page and you can easily be aware of it because of its unique icon which is an arrow that is facing upwards.

Then select your thumbnail after you have finished uploading the video. Actually, YouTube will suggest to you the thumbnails that it thinks that is perfect for your video. However, you can always select the thumbnail according to your own preference by uploading your own created image.

After you have uploaded the video it will give you the privilege to modify it according to your needs.

Video Editing

If you have the urge to still modify the video even if it is already uploaded, the video will be set to private while you are editing it and it will go live again once you finished the editing part.

There are several things that you can do on the image:

- Improve and modify the photo
- Put some concluding screens on it
- Include an extra sound on it
- Caption and card inclusions

It is suggested to utilize captions and cards every time you are making videos. This will result in more interactive videos. It will only take a few moments for you to add them and they are truly worth it.

SEO on YouTube is it Possible?

(Photo reference: https://pixabay.com/photos/digital-marketing-seo-google-1725340/)

We will tackle the benefits of doing it, with the combination of two sites which is YouTube and the most famous search engine in the world that makes it a great way to be searched and to have an online presence that is really decent to be profitable.

YouTube SEO gives out a lot of basic principles as a page where you can optimize straightforwardly. You must do this optimization in these following strategies:

- Include the topmost-ranking keywords to the caption
- Put more keywords in the description part
- Select the proper tags for your uploads, so that they will be visible to search engines

You are not required to put in an astounding title and a super researched keyword since lots of successful videos. Many marketers have found success in using a colon and the keywords after that.

When creating a description, you can attempt to optimize for the most sought keywords, but also extra keywords that you are aware of supporting your campaign.

When looking for keywords, it is suggested to do the analysis for YouTube and its mother company search engine. In this manner, you will have the assurance that your visibility on both is really exceptional, elevating the impressions as high as possible.

Creating High Converting Videos

(Photo reference: https://pixabay.com/photos/edition-video-edit-cut-paste-1677458/)

Your efforts will be wasted if the most important factor in the world is completely overlooked which is the quality of your videos. Whether the content is poorly made or there are no actions that can make the users interactive then expect that you will not get any returns from it. To become successful with your videos you must have this goal of having a commitment to producing videos that people will love.

There are lots of techniques you can utilize to produce videos that are really great when it comes to conversion. Here are the following techniques that you should consider before making that video a reality:

- Producing videos that you have the know people will look for then putting them into a sort of playlist will truly work.
- By putting your uploads on playlists it will become just like a funnel that will make people check out every video that you have in an automated way.

Producing videos that showcase your business as a solution to a certain dilemma that humans experience today.

There's plenty of ways to be resourceful. The secret is to concentrate on your aspirations and produce footages to make them successful.

Always ensure that you have the entrepreneurial mindset, just like what hustler marketers do whenever they are starting their campaigns

CHAPTER 3: BUILDING YOUR LOYAL AUDIENCES

Making Money on YouTube

(Photo reference: https://pixabay.com/photos/money-dollars-success-business-1428594/)

Actually, I do not see anything wrong about monetization on YouTube however, it has certain disadvantages that you are not aware of especially if you are running a specific business. But the good thing is people without any business at all and just doing YouTube for content are the only ones who will benefit from the monetization program

But how did I say so? Since you have this specific niche which is your business itself then most probably if you activate the monetization program of YouTube the chances are there will be ads that will appear on your video that are completely a rival of your business. This itself can actually hurt your business because your audiences might click on the ad link and completely forget your video at all.

So if you are already an established business it could be pretty hard for you to take the risk because you will not get those significant views that easy and the money that you will get from it is not what you expect for. Although there are lots of YouTubers (The people that make a living from YouTube) that are telling that they are earning that much. Yes, it is probably true however before you reach that level it will take you a lot of time as you will need to accumulate hundreds of thousands of subscribers or even millions of it.

However, if you want to make money directly from YouTube itself then content creation is the best for you.

But the aim for most enterprises on this platform is to make money from generating leads, not in the Pay-Per-View(PPV) basis. Aim for this technique, which we have tackled a while ago then you will realize that you will profit much higher in your business than enrolling in any monetization program.

However, there is nothing wrong in activating the monetization program just make it sure that there will be enough subscriber that will wait for the ads to finish so that you can earn money. Since a lot of YouTube audiences just to watch videos and do not want to be disturbed by the ads because that is when

YouTubers earn money although impressions also count it is much bigger earning when an audience finished up your ad.

The Monetization Process

If you come up with a decision that the monetization program is the perfect suit for your enterprise then monetizing it is very easy. You will just have to enable the monetization option and Google will review it if it passed its criteria. Here are the following criteria that they will look at:

- You have read the terms and conditions

- You have set up the monetization options in your settings

- You enabled Adsense

- You have 1,000 subscribers and 10,000 views

After you set up your monetization options, you can already see a number of ads that will come up of your videos then it will prompt you of which one you should only put:

- Skippable advertisements – it is the type of advertisements that run prior to the start of your video

- Overlay ads – this appears on the façade of your videos

- Sponsored ads – this is one of the most flexible ads out there because it can appear on all types of devices that you are using

- Display ads – this usually runs on PC because it appears while the video is running

Availing the Advertisement Services of YouTube

So if you have the urge to utilize ads to make your enterprise known instead of earning money from ads then this is one of the best ones that you can do out there.

Below is the simple guide on how you can actually start advertising on the said platform.

You have to go to YouTube's ad platform page which is very easy to search on Google. YouTube Ads are interconnected with the Google Adwords account that is why if you already have it then it is not required for you anymore to create one.

The Ad producer looks dissimilar than the other social media platforms ads creator looks like. They show up all 4 producing steps on a page, and you must open them to add and modify the content there then check on your video.

You can look for the caption or link of the video that you want to market.

Then place in your ad content and select your thumbnail. Keep in mind that this content is optimized for people to be noticed; it is not a requirement to be a caption.

Know where you desire to put the audiences who press the advertisement. You can transport them to your own YouTube page or to your own blog. In the high percentage of scenarios, transporting viewers to your site is the most effective way to get to your goals.

Then you must put your budget then the platform will start its work for you on a system of bidding and you will only be billed when audiences see the advertisement.

After that, the following step is super crucial because it is the aiming part of the production of your campaign. You can aim regarding place, sexual orientation, age bracket, likes, and many more.

After you have done all those processes then it is now time to submit the form.

Hosting Contests

We are aware of the different contests that social media sites are starting out from time to time. Although it is not as abundant as they are compared to other sites. Because not so many people use them that is why you can definitely use it as an advantage.

Pinterest Marketing

(Photo reference: https://pixabay.com/illustrations/pinterest-icon-symbol-sign-logo-2151052/)

If we are marketing with the use of social media, you would probably take Facebook as your first option. Why digital marketers loved these social media sites is that they are very efficient and easy to use.

But, if you can think creatively and put some spice on everything you do then your enterprise can take advantage of Pinterest as well and I guess this social media site is the most taken for granted among them without them knowing that it is really effective too.

Even though almost half of the population who uses this platform are guys, it's mainly known as a women-filled site because the features tend to be a little bit girlish. This is the primary reason why people just take this for granted.

But not utilizing this wonderful site can really take you away from the many benefits that you can get from it because if you're not utilizing it while using other sites then you are missing out a lot.

The site's statistics are actually growing in numbers that is why this is already on the top social media sites in the world. To tell you honestly, it has done a lot of things when it comes to building site visibility in search engines because of backlinking.

The Meaning of Pinterest Marketing

It is also a social media platform that is derived from the vision of disseminating visuals. The individuals who use this platform are called "pinners" who can arrange, disseminate photos and footage from around the web and look for them too. This gave them the reputation of being one of the best visual social media sites in the world.

Photos and footages that pinners put on the site including the text content are known as pins. They have the privilege of amazingly putting their pins into the pinboards which act as a news feed.

Users can modify and change their boards, which can make people notice and subscribe to you.

The most amazing characteristic of Pinterest is it gives you the privilege to disseminate your thoughts and motivate other people. Furthermore, because every people that are pinning visuals of their own likes and arranging them accordingly, they do not experience any issues with other people viewing their activity.

Why You Have to Opt-in Into Pinterest When it Comes to Marketing?

Pinterest has gone through different ups and downs and they became triumphant through the years. It has transformed to be the epitome of visual social media for many enterprises that has the urge to get traffic back to their site with the use of photos.

The users of this site are well acquainted with searching catchy and amazing products. And they're not a newbie to purchasing an item that they like either through searching or on their pinboard. This is why Pinterest has a greater advantage in increasing the sales of people.

Some Ways to an Efficient Pinterest Marketing

Pinterest is considered a treasure when it comes to marketing. But, achieving success with Pinterest marketing is more than just simply having an extraordinary profile picture and connectivity with friends.

By letting Pinterest advertising work comes down to having a reasonable technique that is aligned with your business objectives. Since at last, constructing a solid profile on Pinterest is just conceivable when you're going the correct way.

Here are some of the different ways you can take advantage of Pinterest showcasing your services and products and grow the scope of your business.

Build Your Authority

There are numerous organizations profiting in different ways by utilizing Pinterest as their marketing medium. One straightforward approach to utilize Pinterest is to manufacture and develop your image expert. This can enable you to get a greater amount of your planned target audience to confide in your image and work with you.

It doesn't make a difference what item or services you are selling, you can generally utilize Pinterest to make more individuals mindful of your image and lead them to purchase from you.

For instance, in case you're in the excellence specialty, you could make a Pinterest photo tutorial that helps and teach ladies to keen on getting an all-out makeover.

The best part is you don't need to create all the posts yourself when pinning. You can adopt a blend and match strategy by sharing from different other definitive sources, which encourages you to show off your business' innovation.

The thought is to give your audiences a feeling that your Pinterest statistics have the spot to discover valuable and dependable data about your industry.

When you assemble your position along these lines, you end up...

- Building trust with your intended interest group and fortify your association with them.

- Experiencing a more elevated amount of client unwavering ness, which can mean recurrent deals over extended periods of time.

- Getting more referrals from satisfied clients and prospects who transform into your reputation promoters.

Grow Your Reach

(Photo reference: https://pixabay.com/illustrations/pinterest-icon-symbol-sign-logo-2151052/)

Let's be honest, each business needs to build its range, since it can prompt greater deals. Having a bigger size group of audiences is likewise the way to testing new items and getting focused on criticism. Pinterest has an exceptionally open network that you can use to connect with a greater arrangement of your crowd.

So as to really develop your arrive in the correct way, you need a procedure at your disposal. Something that isn't normally utilized (or mishandled) by different advertisers.

One such methodology is utilizing your pins. The thought is to go out there and associate with famous Pinterest users who have figured out how to fabricate very effective pins. And afterward, work together with them so you can get your post before the correct target crowd.

This "joint endeavor" gives the benefit to all parties to pick up points of interest from it. You get a higher level of presentation and construct your power by joining forces with a brand that has a high reputation from your industry or niche. Also, they get the chance to impart more incentives to their customers.

Presently, if you need this combined effort to bring results, you need to get in your prospect's shoes and take a view of things from their opinions and preferences. Their supporters ought to be applicable to your posts and the other way around. This joint endeavor should perform well at all levels.

With a touch of vital reasoning, you can rapidly take advantage of a greater portion of your crowd.

Increase Your Traffic

(Photo reference: https://pixabay.com/photos/taxi-vehicle-road-city-urban-cars-1209542/)

Traffic is what is most important to a site. Without the correct sort of traffic coming in, it's just unrealistic to develop your web visibility especially on search engines and increment your online deals. Despite the fact that there are many paid and free approaches to produce important site traffic, Pinterest can leave huge numbers of these techniques when utilized appropriately.

Given the prevalence of Pinterest and the manner in which it has developed, it shouldn't come as an unexpected that it can enable you to get considerably more referral traffic than YouTube and LinkedIn together. So, you won't probably create traffic except if and until Pinterest users do the following:

- See to it that your content is interactive and supportive to share with other people.

- On a daily basis, you must repin your pins

The Pinterest users that have been triumphantly utilizing this site for marketing has the ability to pin amazing visuals to their advantage they aren't disseminating photographs just for their visual charisma but also because they are the amazing parts of content that:

- Decipher dilemmas and solve it eventually

- Motivate individuals to become more efficient

- Present a product or service that is worthy of attention

- Make a stand on a specific hobby

Select Your Keywords

(Photo reference: https://pixabay.com/photos/search-engine-optimization-seo-1359429/)

Individuals search on Pinterest simply just like the manner in which they would on Google. So when making your pins, you have to pick the correct keyword for your themes. Begin by structuring a keyword well only depicts that your intended prospect group of audiences will much attainable.

Decide Your Content Types

One beneficial thing about Pinterest as a visual social mediate set is it's not constrained to static pictures. There is an assortment of types of posts that you can add to your pins to stand out from the group and convey an incentive to your customers. For example:

- Infographics – they are videos that provide a lot of information about a certain matter. They are interactive and creative looking videos mostly cartoons and people love watching at them.

- Animated GIFs – these are funny looking images that move and very entertaining to look at. They catch the attention of people which makes them very great when it comes to building an audience base.

- Footages – short footages are really great and will never go out of business when it comes to social media. It is the material that people want to watch and can gain you a lot of audiences in no time.

So choose previously what content types you'd use for your pins. Do some checking to see what content types are getting the most offers or repins in your niche.

Research Your Competition

In the event that your rivals are dynamic on Pinterest, odds are high that they have their own effective sheets. The thought is to not duplicate what they are doing, yet rather screen their pins to increase knowledge. You're essentially watching out to comprehend their presentation as far as...

- Topics they are picking are getting the results.
- Contents that are unmistakably working for at that point.

It does not mean that you should a stalker to your rivals. Your activity is not just to see what's going on with them or their strengths and weaknesses.

Make a rundown of the content suggestions they are sticking to their pinboards, and break down what content types are helping yourself to have valuable content.

Curate Quality Content

In the event that your board is fresh, you need to ensure it is well utilized to establish great use on building up your audience.

To ensure the initial 10 to 25 pins on the board are top quality and are user-friendly. The pins' content should be...

- Relevant
- Valuable
- Useful

The content you pin ought to urge individuals to check out your boards and in the extended term tail them. As you push ahead, keep producing new and helpful content, and expect to repin any related content that your subscribers do once they discovered that it is helpful.

You can without much of a stretch find and track dependable content sources that follow two fundamental advances:

- Identify any important websites inside your niche that are known to distribute extraordinary content on a reliable premise.
- Discover genuine content that you can share on your new board by visiting communities and other web-based social media just like Reddit, Instagram, and etc.

Keep an Eye on Your Metrics

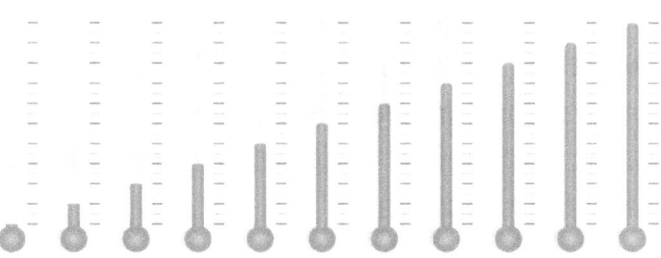

(Photo reference: https://pixabay.com/illustrations/thermometer-temperature-measure-1917500/)

Much the same as some other marketing strategies, you have to realize where you're going with your Pinterest marketing journey. Following your heart, instinct, and understanding will enable you to accomplish better outcomes.

Beginning another board is one of the greatest things that you can take towards your Pinterest marketing journey attempt. What's more? That is actually when you ought to gauge yourself into many desirable results without putting yourself into any kind of risk.

Make sure that you decide the most basic strategies for your Pinterest marketing journey, and utilize the information to comprehend what content sources you should keep utilizing and which you ought to dodge later on.

Simple Yet Powerful Tips to Get Your Pins Noticed

In the event that Pinterest resembles a potential that would work for your business, at that point you have to guarantee that you're not pointing in obscurity. As such, you need to find a way to guarantee your pins get a lot of impressions.

Optimize for Pinterest Search

Getting used to Pinterest turns into much simpler when you have mastered the fundamentals. Since a vast share of dynamic pinners is routinely utilizing the search to discover more pins as possible.

Username

Furthermore, your Pinterest username shouldn't be dealt with like simply one more name. It's a significant component that can enable you to show up in important searches, however, if you practice and utilize it well.

Individuals looking at Pinterest utilize different sorts of terms. Your point is to be shown in searches for the term that is increasingly significant to your image and is likewise well known.

When you have focused on such a keyword, add it to the part of the name. Along these lines, you will possess a superior shot of individuals finding your Pinterest account when they search.

Pin Boards

Regardless of how great your Pinterest pins are, they're not going to profit if your intended group of pinners doesn't get the opportunity to discover them.

Attempt to utilize your essential keywords in the titles of every one of your pins. While individuals may not discover every one of your pins through the searching, despite everything you'll expand your odds of getting found by the correct individuals.

Posted Pins

Think about your pins as a brisk introduction to your visual. Utilizing the correct keywords in your pin posting can enable you to appear in the indexed lists regularly.

A straightforward yet powerful approach to think of watchword thoughts for your portrayal is to type in your root keyword in the Pinterest search box. This ought to consequently give you list the well-known keyword recommendations that individuals are utilizing to look on Pinterest.

Maintain Day-to-Day Consistency

With regards to pinning, you must be consistent because once you are not consistent with your pinning you will constantly lose visibility on search engines not only in Pinterest but in leading search engine websites as well.

- Get more individuals to discover your pins which means more introduction and traffic.

- Boost the number of loyal audiences to your Pinterest account that really likes your pins.

Experiment with Timing

There is no unequivocal recipe with regards to getting your sticking planning right. Contingent upon whether your business is focusing on a nearby group of audiences you ought to consistently explore different avenues regarding your planning when you are pinning stuff.

Likewise, Pinterest is a nice social media site with a wide range of pinners utilizing it. So take time pinning for the duration of the day on various occasions so you're connecting with a greater percentage of your crowd.

Re-pin Older Pins

Picking up focused audiences to your Pinterest stats is just a single piece of the whole scenario. The other part is to really get them to see your pins. The truth of the matter is, not every person is going to see each pin you post. This implies you have to go past normal pinning to get your pins seen and clicked upon.

A trick that is taken for granted most of the time is re-pin and it is truly beneficial for the visibility of your profile. For instance, if there's a pin you posted a month prior that got an incredible reaction, why not re-pin it and get a higher reaction? This should be possible with pins that you posted days, weeks or months prior.

Additional Ways to Promote Your Site for Wider Audiences

Aside from social media, I would like to imprint on your mind that there are more ways to get audiences online just like the following:

- Post in forums – if you have a site that needs to market the next thing that you want to do is to let people know it more. There are lots of communities online that you can utilize to make your website known.

- Answer inquiries on Q and A sites – the site that we are talking about here are Quora and Yahoo! Answers. Although those two are the best ones out there are still other sites that are available but focus on those two first. Answer inquiries that are all related to your niche so that you can drive audiences to your site.

- Join groups on social media sites – there are groups on social media sites such as Facebook and Reddit that you can utilize. Go to their pages and join them then initiate wonderful conversations with them and afterward when your account looks legit already then you can start promoting your site or business but make it not look like an advertisement by having a worthy conversation with people on that site.

So there you go just apply those added techniques and rest assured that you will surely have a rewarding audience-building experience.

Conclusion

There you go that was a great learning experience for you to accumulate the knowledge that you need in order for you to acquire loyal audiences that will help your business grow to a whole new level.

Now you have realized that there are lots of ways for you to get that loyal audience towards you then you must not be afraid anymore of trying out marketing yourself in this digital age. You can have the opportunity to have a much wonderful and satisfying career because you will have a higher chance of meeting your targets.

We have learned that loyal audiences can be acquired through various mediums and as long as you are in the internet world you can utilize as many options as possible. You just have to use it correctly using the right strategy and timing in order for you to succeed. We have come up with the different mediums that you can use in order for you to utilize your campaigns very well.

To sum it up, the following mediums are the following:

- Social media – an example of this are Facebook, Pinterest, and many more, which are the well-known sites that we are using in today's world.

- Offline advertising – the word of the mouth is a strong method in order for your business to be known especially online business because once the news has spread it has a lot of chances to go viral as well.

- Online communities – this medium can be in the form of forums, question and answer sites. This can highly increase the presence of your site in just a short period of time.

Given the fact that you optimized those mediums well it is also a must for you to develop good content if you want the results to be promising. Some of the online marketing options that you can take to make money are the following:

- Affiliate marketing – it is in the form of completing offers, market products either virtual or physical products online and earning a commission from them.

- E-commerce – you can actually sell your very own products online either virtual or physical through various sites and market them accordingly by means of different mediums available.

- Physical store – yes you read it right, a decent online presence will actually give you more customers in the long run.

So that's a brief summary of the important topics that we have tackled a while ago. I hope that you get all the data that you are looking for in order for you to be successful in building that loyal audience as quickly as possible.

www.ingramcontent.com/pod-product-compliance
Lightning Source LLC
Chambersburg PA
CBHW021414210526
45463CB00001B/370